GOOD
HOUSEKEEPING

1,001 AMAZING SCIENCE FACTS

by **Michael Burgan**

with **Rachel Rothman**

Chief Technologist & Executive Technical Director
Good Housekeeping Institute

kids
HEARST
HOME

CONTENTS

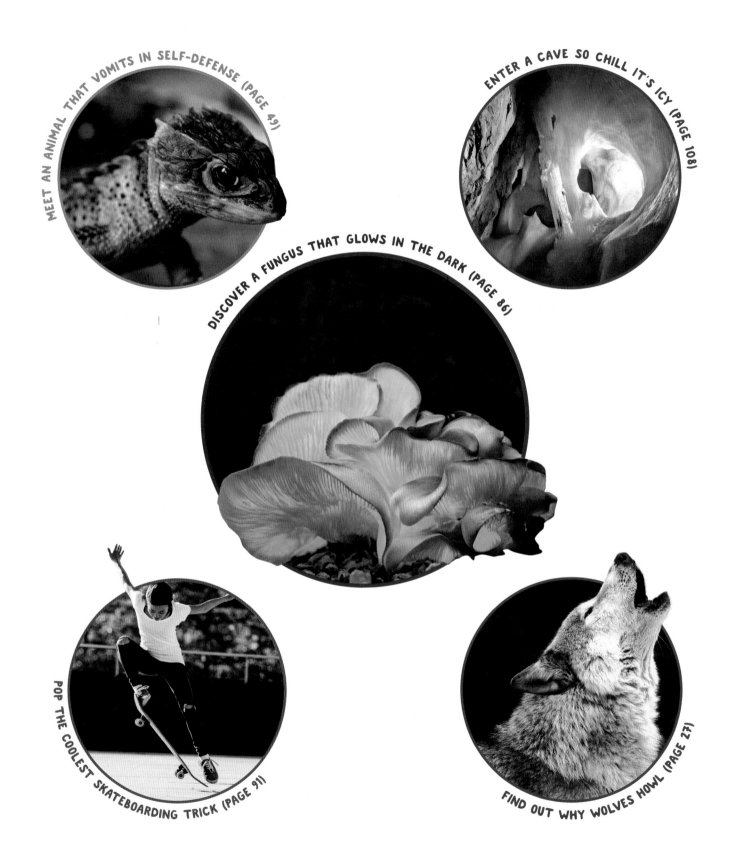

MEET AN ANIMAL THAT VOMITS IN SELF-DEFENSE (PAGE 49)

ENTER A CAVE SO CHILL IT'S ICY (PAGE 108)

DISCOVER A FUNGUS THAT GLOWS IN THE DARK (PAGE 86)

POP THE COOLEST SKATEBOARDING TRICK (PAGE 91)

FIND OUT WHY WOLVES HOWL (PAGE 27)

INVESTIGATE WHAT MAKES SOME FOODS SO STINKY (PAGE 84)

EXPLORE STAR CLUSTERS (PAGE 132)

EAVESDROP ON LIFE IN THE OCEAN (PAGE 151)

Did you know that we drink the same water the dinosaurs drank millions of years ago? That a spacecraft the size of a loaf of bread can orbit Earth using only solar power? And that a single bolt of lightning heats the air around it to five times hotter than the sun?

How do we know these amazing facts? Because of science.

Science helps us understand the world we live in and know how and why things work, and solves the great mysteries of the past. Plus, science enables us to build an incredible future through discoveries and inventions that improve our lives, make it possible for people to live in space, and help us create a sustainable future on Earth.

Dip into *Good Housekeeping 1,001 Amazing Science Facts* to discover the coolest, most incredible facts about animals, nature, the human body, Earth, space, matter (what everything's made up of), chemistry, engineering, and technology. Check out the WOW! and EWW! features, test your science knowledge with cool quizzes, and for some hands-on science, look for a DIY project in each chapter. But most of all, be prepared to *ooh, aah,* and have tons of fun!

RACHEL ROTHMAN
Chief Technologist & Executive Technical Director
Good Housekeeping Institute

BRRR! I USE MY PAWS AND CLAWS TO DIG OUT A DEN FOR A LONG WINTER'S NAP.

BEARS I There are eight bear species. All bears have thick bodies, rounded ears, and shaggy fur, but some characteristics vary. For example, **polar bears** have short, sharp claws designed for gripping ice and slippery seals they hunt. **Brown bears** have longer, curved claws designed to dig for food and pick berries.

Chapter 1

ANIMALS

Thundering elephants, circling sharks, flitting butterflies, and human beings are all animals. There are almost 2 million named species, or distinct kinds, of animals.

Animals live on all the continents and in all the oceans on Earth. From the microscopic water bear to the largest animal on Earth, the giant blue whale, they share some common traits. Let's investigate the vast, diverse, and amazing animal kingdom!

THE ANIMAL KINGDOM

All animals need food to grow and create energy. They all move. And they're all made of more than one cell. Beyond that, some animals are more alike than others and share certain physical traits. About 250 years ago, a scientist named Carl Linnaeus developed a system for naming and classifying, or organizing, animals. He divided the animal kingdom into two groups: vertebrates (animals with spines) and invertebrates (no spines). These groups are further divided into seven main classes, beginning with mammals.

Vertebrates

MAMMALS

Mammals

SPECIES **more than 5,000**

INCLUDES **bears, horses, tigers, whales**

All mammals have hair and three tiny ear bones, feed their babies with mother's milk, and are warm-blooded (they maintain a consistent body temperature that is warmer than their surroundings).

Bats are the only mammals that can fly. Most eat insects, fruit, or a bit of both. Perhaps the most famous are vampire bats. They really do drink blood! But they need only a little at a time and don't hurt the animal "donor." *Phew!*

BIRDS

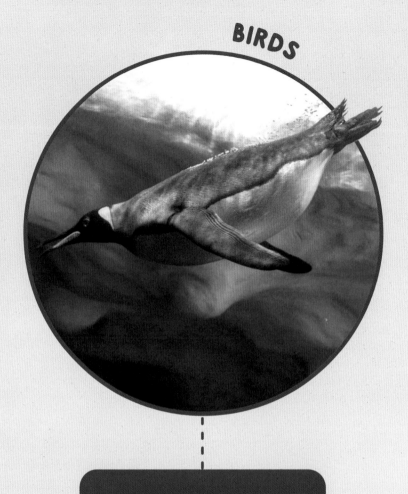

DIY

Birds

SPECIES about 10,000

INCLUDES emus, hummingbirds, owls, penguins

All birds have feathers and wings (though not all birds fly), a beak, hollow bones, special air sacs for breathing, and are warm-blooded. Females lay eggs.

Penguins can't fly, but they can swim and dive—some as deep as 1,500 feet (457 m). That's deeper than the Empire State Building is tall!

BUILD A BIRD FEEDER

This project is for the birds! Tie one end of a piece of twine around a pinecone. Use a craft stick to spread peanut butter or vegetable shortening on the pinecone, then sprinkle it with birdseed. Using the twine, hang your pinecone feeder on a tree branch for your bird buddies to enjoy.

REPTILES

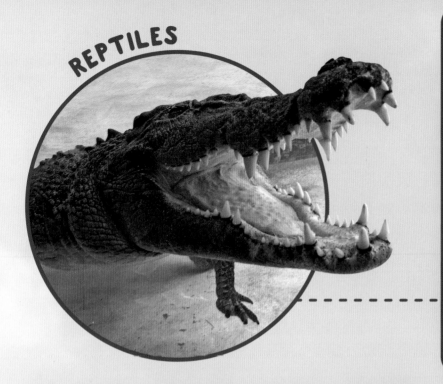

Reptiles

SPECIES about 10,000

INCLUDES **crocodiles, geckos, snakes, turtles**

All reptiles have skin covered with scales or bony plates and are cold-blooded (they can't control their own body temperature; it changes based on their surroundings). Females lay eggs.

The world's biggest reptile is the saltwater crocodile, which can reach 23 feet (7 m) long and weighs more than 1 ton (0.9 mt). That's one-and-one-half times as long as an SUV! A "saltie" hunts by snatching an animal off land and holding it underwater until the prey drowns. Then, it's down the hatch!

Amphibians

SPECIES more than 8,000

INCLUDES **frogs, newts, salamanders, toads**

All amphibians live in or near water, absorb water and breathe air through their skin, and are cold-blooded.

Sometimes it's clear as day how an animal got its name. While glass frogs look green from the top, you can see right through the transparent underside of this species.

AMPHIBIANS

FISH

Fish

SPECIES about 32,000 (more than all the other vertebrate species combined)

INCLUDES **clownfish, goldfish, sharks, tuna**

All fish live in fresh or salty water, have fins for movement, breathe through gills, and are cold-blooded.

In the deep and dark ocean waters, more than 1,500 fish species produce their own light. Some glow down below to say hello; others do it to distract predators. This lanternfish puts on a light show to communicate in deep waters.

Invertebrates

ARTHROPODS

Arthropods

SPECIES about 1,000,000

INCLUDES ants, crabs, spiders, insects

All arthropods have jointed legs and skeletons on the outside of their bodies.

Insects have been on Earth longer than human beings, and some seem like they'll be here forever. Cockroaches can live even after their heads are cut off!

Other Invertebrates

Many other kinds of animals lack a spine but they aren't arthropods. They're a varied bunch, ranging from worms and snails to sea creatures like sponges and octopuses.

Did you know that the octopus has nine brains? They have one big brain in the head and a mini-brain in each of their eight legs. These creatures are incredibly smart. They dig up shells, carry them to a new place, and construct shelters.

OTHER INVERTEBRATES

EWW!

INSECT SOUP

Robber flies grow up to 3 inches (8 cm) long, have spiky legs that help them grab and hold on to a tasty meal, and have beaklike mouthparts. They're also known as assassin flies for the way they hunt and kill prey. After they grab an insect with their legs, they stab it in the back with their beak, inject a venomous saliva that kills the prey and dissolves its insides, and finally they slurp it up. They eat whatever they can catch—beetles, grasshoppers, wasps, and even other robber flies.

SURVIVING AND THRIVING

All animals have basic survival needs that include food and water, a home or other shelter, and oxygen to breathe. But tasty nectar for a bumblebee wouldn't be a meal fit for a shark, and a cozy nest for birds would be way too small for a horse. Each animal needs the right type of of food and shelter, and the right amount of water, to survive.

Yum Some animals eat plants like grasses and leaves (they're called herbivores). There are also fish eaters (piscivores), like **Atlantic puffins**, and meat eaters (carnivores). Animals that sample from a wide buffet of meal options, like most humans, are omnivores ("omni" means all). Herbivores can graze whenever they're hungry. For fish eaters and meat eaters, grabbing a bite often means just that: they hunt for their meal.

Slurp Water is animals' most important need. It keeps them hydrated, helps them eat and digest food, and regulates their body temperature. Some, like a pet cat or an antelope in the African grasslands, slurp it with their tongues. Insects may get water from plants, either from raindrops on leaves or by chewing the greens to release the water inside. Marine mammals live in water, but the ocean is too salty to drink. Instead, they get water from the food they eat. While human beings need to hydrate every day, **camels** can go several weeks without drinking. When they do find water, they can guzzle down 53 gallons (201 l) in just a few minutes.

Take a Breath! Animals take in oxygen, although we don't all breathe in the same way. Land and marine mammals have lungs and breathe in air through their mouth or nose. That blowhole on top of a **whale** or dolphin's head is actually a nostril. Fish and amphibians can get oxygen from water as it passes through their gills or over their skin. And insects breathe through holes on their bodies called spiracles—but they don't have lungs. Scientists have so far found only one living animal that doesn't need oxygen to survive: a parasite that lives in salmon muscles.

Home Sweet Home What is home to an animal? It may be a temporary shelter from bad weather or rough seas, a place to hide out from predators, or somewhere to have and raise babies. Some birds build a new nest each year and others borrow an existing nest. Armadillos and other burrowing animals seek shelter by digging holes underground. Others, like the **rock hyrax**, which lives in shrubby areas, find gaps in rocks or on craggy cliffs. Moray eels make a home in coral reefs, **sea otters** find shelter in protected bays and harbors, polar bears dig snow dens, and squirrels build nests in trees.

WOW!

DEW DROPS

The thorny devil lives in the arid Australian desert, where water is scarce, but morning dew dampens the desert sand. This little lizard has a special way of staying hydrated. It can collect water—including dew—on its skin, that then travels to its mouth.

ONE HABITAT, MANY INHABITANTS

A habitat is like your neighborhood. It has everything an animal needs in one area. Freshwater habitats include rivers, streams, ponds, marshes, and swamps. They support more than 100,000 different kinds of animals around the world. At 1.5 million acres (6,070 sq km), Florida's Everglades is the largest freshwater habitat in the world. Let's take a close-up look at some animals that call this place home.

WOOD DUCKS

MANATEES

The most popular inhabitant in the Everglades is the plump and sweet-looking manatee. It has built-in flotation assistance, with lungs near the top of its body, and it surfaces for air every few minutes. These aquatic mammals, also called sea cows, can weigh more than 3,000 pounds (1,361 kg)—a little more than an average car.

Male wood ducks have brilliantly colored plumage (feathers) during the mating season, which they display to attract a mate. They then molt, shedding their colorful feathers while new, drabber ones grow in. They molt again at the next breeding season, regrowing their brilliant plumage. The females have gray-brown feathers, with white face markings and blue patches on the wings. Southern wood ducks have two broods of ducklings a year, and if females can't find a nest of their own, they share one with another duck.

EYED CLICK BEETLES

No, this insect's spots aren't eyes, but they may scare off predators. If this little acrobat ends up on its back, it can snap itself into the air with a click and flip itself over.

TOKAY GECKOS

These little lizards look like they're happy in their habitat, but they're uninvited guests, also known as an invasive species. Tokay geckos are native to Southeast Asia's rain forest, so how did they get to Florida? These reptiles are sold as pets, and when they escape—or when people abandon them in a natural environment, like a park, wooded area, or swamp—they look for a new home. Experts think that's how tokay geckos became permanent residents of the Everglades.

AMERICAN ALLIGATORS

This swamp-dweller is a keystone species, meaning it is essential to the overall well-being of Its habitat. Females build big nests and lay three dozen or more eggs at a time. After about two months, the hatchlings emerge, and the mother alligator carries them from the nest to the water in her mouth—a delicate process with all those sharp teeth!

15

AGES AND STAGES

Animals go through a life cycle: they're born, grow up and reach the age where they can reproduce, and, eventually, they die. The cycle can be incredibly long or shockingly short.

1. **Birth** Bears have cubs, seals have pups, and human beings have babies. Nearly all mammals reproduce this way, through live birth. But for most animals—all birds, nearly all fish, and most reptiles—reproduction starts with an egg inside the female, which she then lays. Inside that egg, a baby animal grows and, when fully developed, it hatches.

   In some species, the father plays a part in birth. Penguin fathers take turns with the mother sitting on the eggs to keep them warm. And male **seahorses** and sea dragons have a big role to play—they carry eggs in a pouch until the little ones hatch, making them the only animal dads that give birth.

2. **Becoming Adults** Baby animals follow different paths to adulthood. Called maturity, this is the age at which they can reproduce. For a group of mammals called marsupials, that path starts in a pouch on their mother's belly. One pouched animal, the kangaroo, is strong enough to emerge for short periods about six months after birth. 'Roos continue to visit the pouch and stay with their mothers for up to 18 months, until they can survive on their own. For some mammals, it takes just a few months or a year to reach maturity. One type of eel takes up to 20 years to reach maturity, while the turquoise killifish reaches maturity in just 14 days.

   Nearly all insects and some amphibians go through a process called metamorphosis, changing their appearance as they grow from eggs to adults. This is how tadpoles become frogs and caterpillars transform into butterflies. For **mayflies**, it's a group event. These insects start life underwater. After about two years, they go from being nymphs—sort of like teenagers—to adults, all at the same time. Billions of them emerge from water, creating clouds of insects so massive that they show up on National Weather Service radar!

   Those swarming adult mayflies have just one goal—to reproduce—and that happens during their one-day adulthood.

3. **End of Life** Life in the wild can be hard. Some young animals may not have enough food to survive, while others fall victim to predators or accidents. We can't really know how other animals feel at this stage of life, but there's evidence that some animals recognize death. **Elephants** may revisit places where relatives died, seeming to grieve the loss. And crows have loud, squawking "funerals." Or at least that's what they look like. Crows are smart birds, and scientists think they may see a dead crow and realize they need to warn one another about possible dangers.

PRIMATE PARTICULARS

A chimpanzee, a monkey, and an orangutan are all types of great apes, a family of animals that are part of a larger group, or order, called primates. And human beings are primates too.

HUMAN BEINGS

We evolved about 200,000 years ago. Our closest primate relatives are chimpanzees and an ape species called bonobos. We share 98% of our DNA with them. DNA is the inherited molecule in cells of all living organisms that carries traits from generation to generation and determines how each individual looks and grows. We have less hair than other primates, larger brains, smaller jaws and teeth, and our skeletons evolved so we can walk on two feet.

Shared Traits

What do most of the 300 or so primate species have in common?

- Large brains relative to their body size

- Hands or feet that can grasp objects

- Eyesight that is much sharper than their hearing

- Females usually have one baby at a time

- Live long lives, up to 60 or so years (longer for humans)

- Are social creatures and live in groups

SPIDER MONKEY

Does this primate have five limbs? Well, sort of. Its tail is prehensile—that means it can be used like an arm or leg to swing from branch to branch. And there's something else special about it. The same way your fingerprints are different from anyone else's, each spider monkey's tail has a hairless patch that is unlike any other monkey's.

GIBBON

Tra la la! This forest animal wakes up with a song! Gibbons start the day by calling out to one another, making noises that sound like melodies. No one ever has to ask a gibbon to speak up—its song can be heard more than 1 mile (1.6 km) away.

ORANGUTAN

Like other great apes, orangutans build new nests nearly every day, mostly high up in trees. Since they can weigh up to 200 pounds (91 kg), or about as much as a refrigerator, their nests need to be well built and super sturdy. Fortunately, these primates are ace engineers! They weave big branches to form the base of the nest, then add layers of smaller branches and leaves for mattress-like comfort.

CHIMPANZEE

Every day is a spa day for chimps. They're pros at grooming one another, using their hands, mouths, and tongues to search for dirt, bugs, and dead skin. And, yes, they eat any tasty morsels they find! While other primates groom one another, this is a particularly important way chimps form good relationships.

EWW!
THE RUNDOWN

Just like you, gorillas get runny noses. How do they cope? Sometimes they sneeze out the snot or blow it out with a big puff of air. Other times, they take matters into their own hands, using the tried-and-true method—digging in with a finger, investigating, and then taking a taste.

WHAT'S ON THE MENU?

About 25% of all marine creatures live on or visit coral reefs. And they offer an endless buffet for permanent residents and visitors, too. Who eats what, or whom, in this underwater ecosystem is called a food web.

Aquatic Food Web

Animals can fall into more than one group in a food web. For example, tuna are tertiary consumers and are apex (top) predators in a reef world, but when caught for human consumption, they become producers (providing food for people). Switching between roles in this way creates a weblike system.

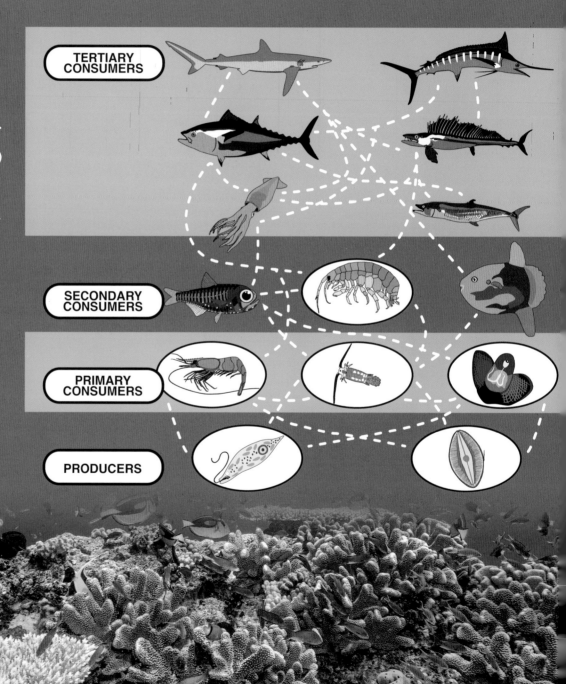

TERTIARY CONSUMERS

SECONDARY CONSUMERS

PRIMARY CONSUMERS

PRODUCERS

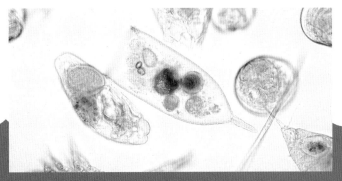

PRODUCERS
The food web starts with plants like seaweed, algae, and animals called phytoplankton. These organisms create their own energy from sunlight and don't consume other creatures. Producers become food for other animals.

PRIMARY CONSUMERS
Zooplankton include coral polyps, tiny snails, and the larvae of some bigger sea creatures, like octopuses. They consume, or eat, producers.

SECONDARY CONSUMERS
Zooplankton become food for fish of all kinds, like snappers, barracuda, and moray eels. Some shellfish, like clams and arthropods (such as shrimp), are secondary consumers, too.

TERTIARY CONSUMERS
The top predators hunt for their food. In a coral reef, these big eaters include reef sharks, hammerheads, and tuna.

How Coral Reefs Form

Coral reefs may look like rocks, but they are actually made up of many tiny sea creatures with exoskeletons (hard shells) that form slowly over thousands, or even millions, of years. They begin when stony or hard coral polyps settle on rocks or other hard surfaces near the shore. They spawn once a year, releasing millions of eggs into the ocean. The eggs become larvae that can attach to existing polyps and produce their own hard shells. This is how coral reefs grow, polyp by polyp, year after year.

LET'S GET MOVING!

People can walk, run, hop, do cartwheels, and get help moving from place to place with a wheelchair, bicycle, car, boat, or plane. Other animals have their own techniques. And some are truly amazing movers.

Land Speed Record **Cheetahs** are the fastest land animal and can zoom along at 60 miles per hour (96.5 km/h)—that's at highway speed for a car! They have long legs to propel them forward and a tail that acts as a rudder for steering. At full speed, all four paws are airborne about half the time.

Slitherin' A flexible body, strong belly muscles, lots of ribs, and strong scales work together to help most snakes glide forward. Tree climbers use an accordion motion, forming their bodies into a zig-zag. They pull forward with the front part and push with the back end. According to the Guinness World Records, the fastest land snake is a tree climber, the **black mamba**, which clocks in at up to 12 miles per hour (19 km/h).

SNAKE SCALES ARE MADE OF KERATIN. THAT'S THE SAME THING THAT MAKES YOUR HAIR AND FINGERNAILS STRONG.

Airborne Insects, bats, and most birds use wings to fly. Some things with wings prefer to walk. Roadrunners, birds that live in the southwestern United States, can dash along at up to 25 miles per hour (40 km/h), twice as fast as your bicycle goes. And most cockroaches walk rather than fly—phew! The fastest flier is the **peregrine falcon**. In a dive called a stoop, it travels at more than 200 miles per hour (322 km/h) to catch its prey. That's as fast as a bullet train.

The High Life How do animals that spend a lot of time in trees get from one branch to another? A **gibbon** uses its arms and hands to swing through the trees and can move as fast as a person can run! Flying squirrels don't really fly—they have skin flaps between their front and back legs that help them glide through the air from branch to branch. And some tree dwellers have special feet that help them walk up a tree. Gecko feet have millions of tiny hairs that help them stick to almost any surface—even a ceiling!

Keep On Swimming Fish have tails and fins to move through water. Whales and dolphins use their flippers the way fish use their fins. And penguins—non-fliers in the bird world—use their wings like flippers to travel through the water. The speedster in the water is the **sailfish**. It folds down its fins to create a super sleek torpedo-shaped body and zips along at 67 miles per hour (108 km/h). And most sharks can't ever stop swimming—they need the oxygen from the water passing through their gills to survive.

REMARKABLE RELATIONSHIPS

Why would a tiny frog and a fanged tarantula hang out together? These very different animals actually help each other out. Let's look at how they, and other animals, interact in ways that scientists call symbiosis. Sometimes both animals benefit, and other times, well . . .

Competition

When resources are limited, animals of different species may have to compete for food, water, or shelter. This can be especially harmful when an invasive species—an animal not native to the habitat—is introduced. Sometimes invasive species are pets gone wrong: Burmese pythons that got WAY TOO BIG were released into the Everglades, where they are top predators that alter the natural balance of the habitat.

Mutualism

In the Amazon, a slick-skinned humming frog and a hairy tarantula share a burrow or hole, and both benefit from their relationship. The frog eats bugs that might want to dine on the spider's eggs, thus protecting the eggs from harm. In turn, the spider protects both her offspring and the small frog from predators.

Predation

This type of symbiosis is a one-way street! Predators hunt prey to eat, and prey get eaten. This helps big animals, like orcas, which consume more than 100 other animal species. Not all predators are huge. Owls, raccoons, and ladybugs hunt prey, too.

Parasitism

The host in this type of relationship is definitely the loser to the parasite. Parasitic animals live on, with, or even inside host animals. Some wasps lay eggs on a caterpillar or inject them under the skin. When the eggs hatch, the larvae eat the caterpillar before emerging as adults.

Commensalism

Sometimes, only one animal gets help, with no benefit or risk to the other. Take the cattle egret, a bird that uses livestock (the host) to help them find food. As the host walks through a field of grass, it reveals bugs, which the egret eats. The egret also rides on the host's back and snacks on bugs on its skin.

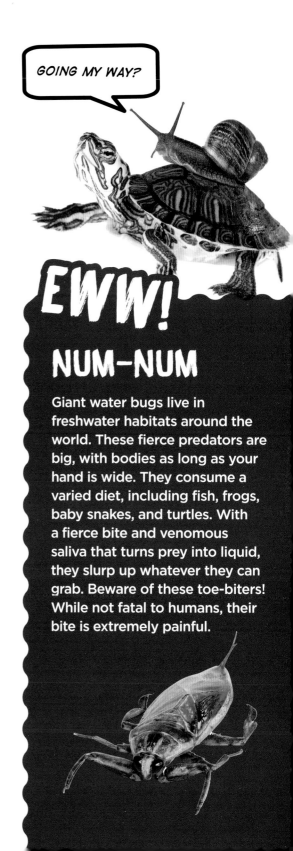

GOING MY WAY?

EWW!
NUM-NUM

Giant water bugs live in freshwater habitats around the world. These fierce predators are big, with bodies as long as your hand is wide. They consume a varied diet, including fish, frogs, baby snakes, and turtles. With a fierce bite and venomous saliva that turns prey into liquid, they slurp up whatever they can grab. Beware of these toe-biters! While not fatal to humans, their bite is extremely painful.

WOLF! WOOF!

More than 69 million American households have at least one dog, making dogs the most popular pet. But people and dogs weren't always so close. Our pups descended from a fierce wild animal, the wolf.

About 15,000 years ago, when people survived by hunting and foraging for edible plants, wild wolves began hanging around hunting camps, where food was plentiful when people tossed out scraps. Some of the wolves were friendlier than others, and humans saw the value of having them around. These more approachable animals acted as "watchwolves," alerting people to danger. Over time, people began mating tamer male and female wolves. They chose wolves with specific behaviors, abilities, sizes, shapes, and coat colors. Their offspring eventually evolved into dogs, the first animals that people domesticated, trained as working animals, and took in as close human companions.

Let's take a closer look at the similarities and differences between wild wolves and domesticated dogs.

Characteristics	WOLVES	DOGS
Social	🐾	🐾
Live in packs in the wild	🐾	
Form extended family groups with other wolves	🐾	
Aggressively protect their territory	🐾	
Have a strong sense of smell	🐾	🐾
Are highly intelligent and can learn new behaviors quickly	🐾	🐾
Can mark a scent, called a pheromone, onto another wolf to make it part of its family	🐾	
Naturally bond with people		🐾
Form extended family groups with other animals and people		🐾
Some breeds aggressively protect or guard		🐾
Can be trained to help people, from guiding sightless people around, to becoming guard and police dogs, to herding sheep		🐾

A SIBERIAN HUSKY CAN RUN MORE THAN 100 MILES (161 KM) A DAY!

TIMBER WOLF

Wolves howl to let other pack members know where they are, to call far-ranging pack members together, and as a warning to rival wolf packs.

I NEED A REST!

ARCTIC WOLF

WOW!
SPEEDSTERS

What do greyhounds and cheetahs have in common? They're both the fastest of their kind! Both of these animals achieve their high speeds by contracting and extending their bodies, with all four legs off the ground part of the time. Unlike the cheetah, which can only put on short bursts of speed, a greyhound can run at 35 miles per hour (56 km/h) for up to 7 miles (11 km), and it can go even faster for shorter sprints.

CLEVER CATS

The kitty that purrs on your lap is descended from the North African wildcat, wild felines that experts think were domesticated about 12,000 years ago. That's when people increasingly lived in villages and farmed the land. People saw that cats were "purr-fect" for controlling pesky pests like mice and other rodents, and some began feeding the cats to make sure they stuck around. Today, more than 45 million American households have at least one pet cat.

Fantastic Felines

Cats are famous for fabulous balance, a twisty spine, and an ability to right themselves in midair and land on their feet. They're also incredibly curious creatures, which means they may risk a giant leap or an accidental fall. This trait stems back to their wild days when they spent a lot of time in trees. Cats are still excellent tree climbers.

A cat's whiskers are like kitty radar—they help cats navigate their way through the world. Found on the cheeks, over the eyes, above the lips, and even on the front legs, whiskers send signals to the cat's brain about vibrations and air currents, which help the cat know how far away something is, whether it can fit through a narrow gap, how its body is oriented, and even whether it has a firm grip on its prey.

Cats can turn each ear independently to detect where a sound is coming from—a useful skill for hunting. They also communicate with their ears. When they're calm and contented, the ears are relaxed and face forward. Straight up and facing forward is the alert position—your cat is trying to take in information. And if the ears are flattened and sideways, like the wings of an airplane, the cat is frightened or upset and wants to be left alone.

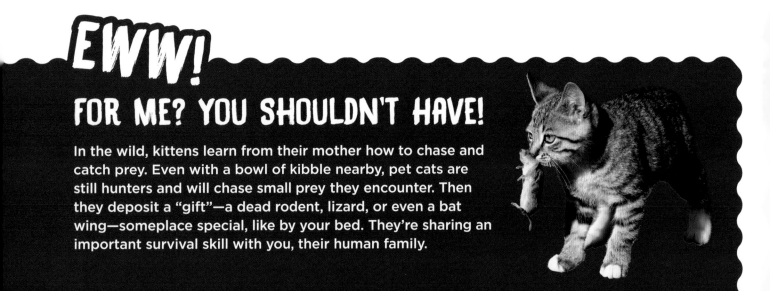

EWW!
FOR ME? YOU SHOULDN'T HAVE!

In the wild, kittens learn from their mother how to chase and catch prey. Even with a bowl of kibble nearby, pet cats are still hunters and will chase small prey they encounter. Then they deposit a "gift"—a dead rodent, lizard, or even a bat wing—someplace special, like by your bed. They're sharing an important survival skill with you, their human family.

QUIZ

THAT'S WILD . . . OR IS IT?

Domesticated cats share some traits with their wild cat relatives. See if you know how they're alike and how they're different with these true-or-false statements.

1. ALL CATS PURR.

2. ALL CATS LIKE TO SCRATCH THINGS.

3. ONLY DOMESTICATED CATS MEOW.

4. ALL CATS HISS BUT THEY CAN'T GROWL.

Answers are on page 156.

SAY WHAT?

Animals don't need words to communicate. They have their own ways of saying "Hey, come this way" or "Back off!"

Spitting cobras shoot streams of venom to say, "Go away!" They aim for the eyes to blind their victim. They can spit up to 6 feet (1.8 m) with amazing accuracy.

If you get too close to a **skunk**, it will arch its back, turn its backside toward you, and stamp its feet. If you don't take the hint, you'll be hit with a stinky spray that shoots out from glands on the skunk's butt. Like rotten eggs, it has sulfur in it, which smells really, really bad. Skunk spray can reach up to 20 feet (6 m) away.

Some animals use color to communicate. The venomous **blue-ringed octopus** has an incredible built-in warning system—it lights up with glowing blue rings all over its body when threatened. This self-defense tactic lets others know that while they're small, these eight-legged creatures are dangerous to try to eat.

An **alpaca** is a masterful spitter, launching a stream to make another animal back off. A female will spit to tell a male she's not interested. The liquid comes from the stomach and is more like vomit than saliva. After spitting, the animal will often munch on a leaf to get the terrible taste out of its own mouth.

Honeybees move to the groove, wiggling their butts in a little dance. Some wiggles are called waggles, and these tell other bees where to find flowers filled with nectar or pollen. Sometimes multiple bees have a waggle competition over which one found the best food source, hoping they're the winning bee that waggles, "Follow me!"

EWW!

GET THE SCOOP FROM POOP

Some animals get information from other animals' leavings. White rhinos share a bathroom of sorts, pooping in the same big ol' pile. This dung heap acts like a community bulletin board: chemicals in a white rhino's poop give other rhinos useful information, such as how old the pooper is and if it's looking to mate.

THAT STINKS!

BUG BLASTS

For **BEARDED LACEWING** larvae, farting is more than a way to pass gas. It helps them catch their dinner! A blast of the insect's gas can stun up to six termites at once. The fart leaves the termites unable to move for up to three hours, giving the lacewing plenty of time to chow down.

FART-FREE

Do all animals fart? Nope. Sloths don't fart, and almost all birds are tootless. That's most likely because the **BIRDS'** digestive systems don't have the right kind of bacteria to create gas. But they're pros at pooping— some species let 'er rip every few minutes!

STOMACH RUMBLES

COWS are double trouble when it comes to gassy emissions. They're ruminants, a group of mammals that includes goats, sheep, buffalo, camels, and giraffes. These animals have four-chambered stomachs and digest food multiple times. Ruminants produce methane—a greenhouse gas that contributes to global warming—and it comes out from both ends. It also enters the atmosphere from their manure.

GET GASSY TOGETHER

Farting can be more than a way to pass gas. For **HERRING**, farts may be a way to "talk" to each other. The little fish release gas, making a distinct sound in the process. Some scientists think the farting is one way herring know to swim together in dark waters.

TELLTALE SMELL

Farts begin when bacteria in the gut break down food and gas builds up and the trapped air comes out. Whether—and how bad—a fart smells has to do with the food an animal eats. **ELEPHANTS**, rhinos, and hippos munch on grasses that take a long time to break down during digestion. Eventually, there's too much gas to hold in. When one of these big beasts lets it rip at the zoo, the sound of their thunderous farts gets everyone's attention.

TOOT AND SCOOT

The gas animals pass isn't always gut-related. **SONORAN CORAL SNAKES** take in air through their butts, then fart it out again, creating a noise that scares away predators.

HAVASUPAI FALLS | The stunning turquoise color of Havasupai Falls in Arizona comes from a high level of calcium carbonate in the rocks. This common mineral is also found in eggshells, coral, and even your teeth and bones.

Chapter 2

NATURE

What do sweet peaches, tall trees, majestic mountains, roaring rivers, and spring showers have to do with one another? They're all part of nature, or our physical world. Nature includes materials people use, like wood from trees and honey from bees. It's where people and animals and insects hang out, from sandy shores to city parks. It's up, down, and all around you. You're part of nature too!

YOUR HOME IS A BIOME

Can a furry polar bear live in the toasty tropical rain forest? Would a winter-loving pine tree be happy in a desert? Why is it tough for any creature to tunnel in the tundra? Biomes hold the answers to all those questions. That's the scientific term for a group of plants and animals that share a climate and terrain. Cool fact: your body is a biome, too, with all kinds of living creatures inside you (more about that in Chapter 3)!

GRASSLANDS

What you find in the **grasslands** biome is right there in the name—grass on lots of land. Grasslands are great places for animals to graze: think of bison on the American prairie and elephants on the African savanna. Temperate grasslands have hot and cold seasons, and tropical ones have rainy and dry seasons.

WHERE CAN YOU FIND AN OCEAN WITH NO WATER?

AQUATIC

No deep digging here! **Tundras** are extremely cold and very dry, and the sun may not shine for weeks during the long winter months. The ground is frozen most of the time, but a short summer season allows the topsoil to thaw just long enough for some plants to grow. Polar bears are white to blend in with the snowy tundra. Or are they? Their fur is actually clear—the reflection of the light makes it look white.

ON A MAP!

The biggest and the wettest one, the **aquatic** biome, has two main parts. One is called marine—that's where the water is salty. The other is freshwater, such as streams and rivers.

Did you know? This biome covers 70% of Earth's surface. There's WAY more water than land on our planet.

FOREST

Trees dominate the **forest** biome, which has three main variations:

- **Taiga** (TY-gah) has hardy evergreens like pine, spruce, and fir trees. There is year-round precipitation, with plenty of snow during long, cold winters.

- **Temperate forests**, with four seasons, are home to trees that shed their leaves every year, like oak, maple, and cottonwood. Fallen leaves decompose quickly with the help of insects and other organisms, adding nutrients to the soil.

- **Tropical forests**, also known as rain forests, are warm and damp. They have the greatest diversity of plant and animal species on Earth.

Did you know? Rain forests are buggy places! One study found more than 6,000 species of insects in a single acre of a rain forest in Panama, an area smaller than an American football field.

DESERT

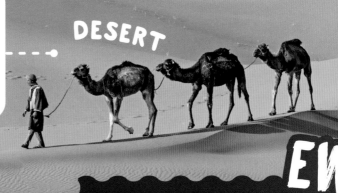

Does the word **desert** make you think of the hot and dry Sahara or Mojave Deserts? Believe it or not, cold and icy Antarctica is also a desert—it rains very little there, too. The lack of rainfall and the extreme temperatures mean deserts have much less plant and animal life than other biomes.

TUNDRA

EWW!

FOUL FLOWERS

Skunk cabbage smells really, really bad. It releases a stinky aroma when it blooms and when its leaves are crushed. It sounds gross, but this stench actually helps attract pollinators. It also keeps away animals that might step on it. Native to North America, this ripe-smelling plant grows in wet, swampy areas.

LAND HO!

When you hike up a hill on a rocky trail, ski down a snow-covered slope, or follow a tree-lined path in a city park, you're walking on land. This solid part of Earth's surface comes in different shapes and sizes. Land always contains rocks, soil, and elements of Earth's crust.

Mountains Tall peaks form when pieces of Earth's crust called tectonic plates crash into one another. The force pushes the crust upward, creating a mountain or a mountain chain. Tectonic plates move VERY slowly—mountain-making can take millions of years!

At 29,032 feet (8,849 m), **Mount Everest**, in the Himalaya mountain range, is the tallest peak on Earth. That's the equivalent of about 300 ten-story buildings stacked on top of one another.

Hills Smaller than mountains, hills can have peaked (pointed) or rounded tops. Often, hills form in a chain, separated by low areas called valleys.

Wind, rain, and erosion helped shape the **Painted Hills** in Oregon. It may look like an artist added the colorful stripes, but the different layers were formed by cycles of changes over millions of years: hot, cold, wet, and dry.

MOUNT EVEREST

PAINTED HILLS

Plains Found on every continent, these large, relatively flat places are formed over time by layers of snow that turn to ice, volcanic lava that spreads out over surrounding land, or flooding rivers that leave mud and silt behind when the waters recede (go down). The **Great Plains** of North America cover more than one-third of the United States (and parts of Canada, too).

GREAT PLAINS

TIBETAN PLATEAU

Plateaus These expansive, flat, elevated places are formed by the collision of tectonic plates. The largest is the **Tibetan Plateau**, at 965,000 square miles (2.5 million sq km). That's more than three and a half times as large as Texas, the largest U.S. state! It is located between Mount Everest and K2, in a region known as "the roof of the world" because it is the highest land area on Earth.

EWW!
INSECT EFFECT

What's going on underfoot? Termites, cockroaches, and millipedes feast on decaying plant matter in the soil. As they digest food, they, um, fart. They also poop, adding nutrients back to the soil.

TOP SEED

A tiny seed contains every part of a plant inside it. Add good soil, light, air, enough room, the right temperature, water, nutrients, and plenty of time, and it becomes a beautiful plant.

1. Plants take in sunlight, water, and carbon dioxide from the air and convert them into oxygen and energy, supplied in a form of sugar called glucose. The plants then release the oxygen into the air and store the energy in tiny structures, called **chloroplasts,** within plant cells. A pigment within the chloroplasts called chlorophyll, gives plants their green color. This process is called photosynthesis (foh-toh-SIN-thi-sis).

2. Plants collect some moisture from the air, but they get most of their water from the soil, absorbing it through their roots. Water travels up the plant to the leaves, where it is released back into the air as vapor. This process is called **transpiration**.

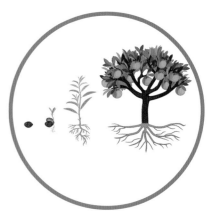

3. Plants take in nutrients—such as carbon, hydrogen, nitrogen, phosphorus, and potassium—from soil and air. If a plant gets too few nutrients, it won't be able to grow properly. This is also true if a seed is planted in soil with too many nutrients—such as more nitrogen than it needs—or if a grower adds too much fertilizer. Through photosynthesis, the **small seed grows** into a sprout, then a sapling, and finally a full-grown plant.

QUIZ

DID YOU KNOW?

Botany is the scientific study of plants. Botanically speaking, fruits contain seeds and vegetables are the roots, stems, and leaves of plants. That seems clear enough. But when it comes to which is which, things can get complicated. Can you guess which are fruits and which are veggies?

1. AVOCADO

2. GREEN BEANS

3. OLIVES

4. RHUBARB

5. SPINACH

6. WATERMELON

Answers are on page 156.

SOW AND GROW

A giant pine tree, a goat, and a wispy strand of wheat all need nutrients (food), land, water, air, and sunlight to grow. And they are also important resources for people. Trees become wood for building houses and furniture, goats provide milk for drinking and making yogurt and cheese, and wheat is turned into flour for pasta, pizza, and—most important—cookies!

Better Together Agriculture generally means growing plants for food. Forestry, a type of agriculture, means growing trees for harvesting. When farmers do both, that's called agroforestry. Sometimes animals such as goats, sheep, and egg-laying chickens are also raised on an agroforestry farm. Let's see how this is good for people, crops, animals, and the planet.

1. **Stops Big Wind Damage** A coat called a windbreaker is made of wind-resistant fabric, so it protects you on a windy day. Creating windbreaks with trees is a way farmers can protect their crops and animals. Windbreaks help stop high winds from damaging delicate crops and blowing away healthy soil.

2. **Helps Water and Land** Riparian buffers are rows of trees planted along riverbanks. Their branches slow down the rate at which rain reaches the ground, and they spread raindrops across a wider area. This helps prevent soil erosion and reduces the likelihood that a river will overflow and cause a flood.

3. **Protects Livestock** When livestock farmers plant trees in grazing fields, animals have it made in the shade—literally. Trees provide cool shade in summertime heat. As a bonus, grazing livestock—animals that eat plants, like cows, pigs, and sheep—can please the trees. Their poop is a form of fertilizer that helps the trees grow.

4. **Fights Climate Change** When farmers plant trees along with their crops, they're helping the planet. Too much carbon dioxide in the air contributes to global warming. Trees to the rescue! They suck up carbon dioxide through their leaves and convert it to food, which helps slow the planet's rising temperatures. Trees also make soils healthy, helping them to absorb carbon dioxide.

Go, plants! Scientists estimate that plants absorb 25% of the carbon dioxide produced by using fossil fuels (such as gas and coal) and release oxygen that we need to breathe.

MARCH 21

A Tree-mendous Day!

Trees are huge helpers to life on Earth. They release oxygen into the air, their branches offer shelter from the elements, and they provide food for people and other living things. The United Nations designated March 21 as the International Day of Forests. How are trees important to you?

POLLINATION STATION

When a bee travels from flower to flower, it's looking for sweet nectar. While it sips and slurps, it also picks up flower pollen, which is sticky and attaches to its body. When it lands on the next flower, some of the pollen drops off. In this way, pollen is transferred from one flowering plant to the pistil of another. (A pistil is the reproductive part of a flower.)

More than three-quarters of all flowering plants—including most fruits and vegetables—reproduce with assistance from animals, including birds, bats, and rodents. And by far, the greatest helpers are insects. They take care of an amazing 90% of all flowering plant pollination.

Seed Dispersal

Blown Away A fluffy dandelion top blown by the wind is spreading—or dispersing—its own seeds.

Carried Away In a kind of scavenger hunt, squirrels look for acorns they buried to eat during cold winter months. Seeds inside any forgotten acorns can grow into oak trees.

Pooped Away When a bear eats berries, it deposits undigested seeds (with a helping of manure fertilizer) when it poops.

WOW!

TOP POLLINATOR AWARD

Announcing the winners: honeybees, bumblebees, butterflies, moths, and beetles. These superstars are the most productive pollinators among the thousands of insects that keep wildflowers, gardens, crops, and orchards growing.

DO BEES POOP?

YES! HONEY-BEE POOP IS YELLOW!

DIY

MAKE A BEE WATERING STATION

Bees are great fliers, but they can't swim. They need a safe place to perch while they drink water.

To make a bee watering station, all you need is a few simple supplies: a large plant saucer, clean stones or marbles, and water.

Place the plant saucer on a tree stump, bench, or table—someplace where other animals won't easily get to it. Fill it with stones or marbles and add enough water to almost cover the stones. Check the water level every few days and add more as needed.

THE WATER CYCLE

Water is always on the move, with the help of the sun. Heat energy from the sun changes water from its liquid state to a gas, or vapor. When the water loses enough of this energy, it turns into a solid—snow. The cycle of water in the atmosphere is called transportation.

Evaporation The sun's heat warms up all forms of water into vapor, which then rises into the atmosphere. This is how puddles evaporate after a rain shower and snow melts on a sunny day. Evaporation is like built-in air-conditioning: it dries the sweat on your skin and cools you off in the process.

Condensation High in the sky, where temperatures are cold, some of the water vapor turns into liquid and ice. These cling to dust and other tiny bits of matter, forming clouds.

Precipitation When enough water or ice come together in a cloud, we're going to get wet! Depending on the temperature of the air and land, droplets fall as rain, snow, hail, or sleet.

WHEN YOU PERSPIRE, YOU TRANSPIRE YOUR SWEAT.

WOW!

WHAT'S IN THAT RAINDROP?

Rain comes from water that started in the ocean, which makes us wonder, do fish pee in the ocean? Yes! Does that mean rain, which started out as evaporated ocean water, contains fish urine? No! Only the water itself turns to vapor and enters the water cycle.

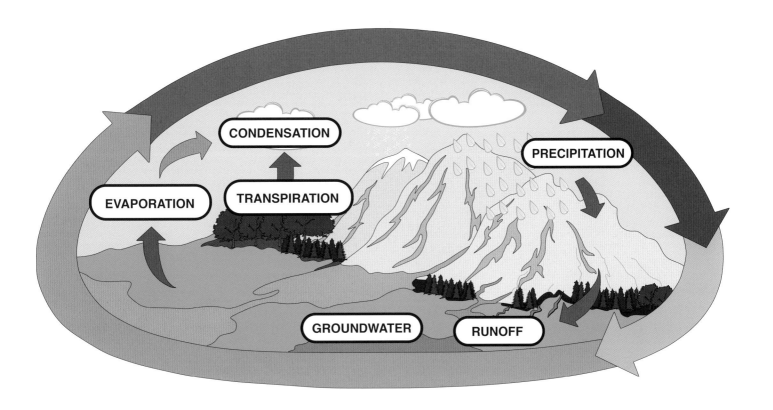

H₂O Is on the Go

Plants can't live without water—and neither can you! Fortunately, it's everywhere around us, filling oceans and rivers, and in the damp soil beneath our feet.

Oceans The greatest source of water that the sun's energy can convert into vapor is our oceans, seas, and other salty bodies of water.

Runoff Rainwater, as well as melted ice and snow, flows down from high spots like mountains and hills. When there is enough runoff, it can form a stream, which may meet up with a river. Eventually, all rivers flow into the ocean.

Groundwater You can't see it and you won't get wet, but there's a lot of water flowing beneath your feet. Worldwide, about 30% of all fresh water is groundwater. Groundwater is always on the move, and some of it ends up in ponds, lakes, streams, and rivers.

Transpiration Plants pass water out through tiny holes in their leaves called stomata. It evaporates into the atmosphere in a process is called transpiration. One large oak tree can transpire 40,000 gallons (151,000 l) a year. That's enough for 25,000 toilet flushes—a 13-year supply!

WET AND WILD

Rain forests earn their name! They get about 80 to 400 inches (203 to 1,016 cm) of rainfall in a typical year, depending on the location. By comparison, the average rainfall in the United States is about 30 inches (76 cm). Rain forests are the wettest and wildest places on Earth, home to millions of plant and animal species.

There's a small island off the northern coast of Australia called New Guinea that has the third-largest rain forest in the world (after the Amazon and Congo). It's important because it's home to 5% of all known animal and plant species, two-thirds of which live only on this island. Let's meet some of its unique inhabitants.

MATSCHIE'S TREE KANGAROO

This is not your usual 'roo! These little cousins of the big kangaroos spend most of their time living the high life. Energetic when awake, they use their strong limbs and bark-gripping claws to move swiftly among the tall trees, looking for tasty ferns and flowers to eat. They curl up in tree branches to sleep for more than half the day.

QUEEN ALEXANDRA'S BIRDWING

A butterfly as big as a bird? Believe it! With a wingspan of 1 foot (30.5 cm), this butterfly is the largest in the world. That's more than twice as big as a hummingbird. It flits around and can be found in the rain forest canopy (high up, where branches and leaves overlap) or closer to the ground.

RED-EYED CROCODILE SKINK

With pointed scales running down its back, this armored lizard resembles a mini crocodile. But it doesn't have the croc's fierce teeth or jaws, so when threatened, it may resort to yelping, vomiting, shedding its tail (which keeps moving, distracting a predator), or even playing dead.

KLINKI PINE

You have to look up, way up, to see the top of the tallest tree in the forest. At almost 300 feet (91.4 m), the klinki pine is nearly as tall as the Statue of Liberty. It grows higher than the forest canopy and produces cones that hold edible seeds that look like nuts.

RAGGIANA BIRD-OF-PARADISE

This native bird is about 13 inches (33 cm) long, but that's just the head and body. Its tail can grow to 3 feet (.92 m) long! To attract a mate, the males have a dance competition, bobbing their heads and fanning out their feathers in noisy and dramatic displays. This colorful and dramatic creature is Papua New Guinea's national bird.

WOW!

FRESH AIR

Rain forests are good for the planet's health! They breathe in carbon dioxide (CO_2) from the air and breathe out oxygen, cleaning the air of excess CO_2 and replacing it with oxygen we need to survive. This, a part of the process called photosynthesis, is important because too much CO_2 contributes to global warming, trapping the sun's energy in our atmosphere and overheating the planet. Rain forests also play a big part in the water cycle. The transpiration of plants in tropical forests creates rain clouds that travel around the world.

THE PROBLEM WITH PLASTIC

The amount of trash in our oceans has grown to epic proportions. There are five huge areas, called patches, where it collects. The biggest is the Great Pacific Garbage Patch, located between California and Hawaii. It covers about 617,000 square miles (1.6 million sq km)—an area almost as big as Alaska.

Most ocean garbage, called marine debris (duh-BREE), is plastic—plastic bags, fishing nets, and water and soda bottles. Some tiny pieces, called microplastics, are so small you can barely see them.

Experts estimate more than 8 million tons (7.3 million mt) of plastic enter the ocean annually—that's more than 53,000 blue whales weigh. Scientists estimate that plastic makes up 80% of all marine debris. Below are the numbers of items removed by volunteers around the world on a single day during an annual International Coastal Cleanup.

224,270
straws

627,014
bottles

272,399
bags

From Park to Patch

To get to the ocean, trash is carried by wind, stream, river, storm drain, and sewer. Let's follow the journey of a single item.

1. The recycling bin at the park is full, so a plastic bottle ends up in the trash.
2. The next day, the trash is collected and taken to the dump. It ends up in an area called landfill, where all solid waste goes.
3. A gust of wind carries the plastic bottle to a nearby stream, where it floats until it reaches a river. The river empties into the ocean, taking the bottle with it.
4. Ocean currents carry the bottle out to sea. Rotating currents called gyres drag it and other plastics farther into the ocean, making the garbage patch grow.

EVERYONE CAN HELP RECYCLE—FROM COMPANIES TO GOVERNMENTS, EVEN YOU AND ME!

WHO, ME?

EWW!

MICRO MESS

Microplastics are all around, from the top of Mount Everest to house dust on floors. They come from materials people produce and use, like nylon fabrics and cleaning scrubbers. And when marine debris such as fishing nets and plastic bottles decompose, microplastics remain in the ocean.

THE THREE Rs

Recycling bins usually have a three-sided emblem that represents three important ways we can help our planet when it comes to plastics and other disposable materials: reduce, reuse, and recycle. Governments, corporations, schools, and individuals can all make decisions that help us use less stuff, repurpose more, and do our bit to save the planet.

Reduce

Think about ways people can reduce the use of natural resources like food and water and see if any fit into your daily life.

Food Did you know that one-third of food produced for people to eat is thrown away or lost due to poor storage? If your family is throwing away uneaten groceries, consider making a chart to track how much is bought, eaten, and tossed each week. Try this for a few weeks and see if you notice any patterns, such as food bought to prepare for dinners that ends up getting lost in the back of the fridge. If it's hard to remember what's in the fridge, keep a list—that way, you can snack on tasty cucumbers rather than toss out rotten ones that have sat too long.

Water A 10-minute shower uses about 40 gallons (151 l) of water. A water-conserving showerhead reduces this amount by 60%. Letting the water run while brushing your teeth uses about 5 gallons (19 l) of water. Whoa! That's 80 cups of drinkable water going down the drain. And turning the water off when you wash your hands uses up to 75% less than leaving it running.

Can you think of other ways to make a daily difference?

Reuse

Secondhand clothes are one cool way to help the planet. Reused clothes save energy and materials needed to make new items, save fuel that would have been used to go on a shopping trip, and cut down on the garbage headed for your local landfill. Are there other ways you and your family might start to reuse things instead of throwing them away?

Recycle

How to make clothing from recycled and sustainable materials is taught on some college campuses. A Michigan college student even started a company that uses plastic waste to make T-shirts. And each year in Florida, teens use recycled trash to make clothing that is featured in a Young at Art fashion show. The theme in 2022 was Oceans Restyled.

Made from repurposed denim jeans, this sculpture—called Messy—was inspired by Nessie, the mythical Loch Ness monster. It was displayed in London to raise awareness about climate change.

↓

WHAT DO YOU CALL A GROUP OF BABY GARBAGE CANS?

A LITTER!

SEVEN WONDERS OF THE NATURAL WORLD

Located off the coast of Rio de Janeiro in Brazil, this is the largest natural bay in the world. Guanabara Bay's surface area is 159 square miles (412 sq km), which is four times as big as Disney World. There are more than 100 islands in the bay, which also has beaches and sailing marinas. This was the site of sailing competitions during the 2016 Rio Olympic Games.

GUANABARA BAY

GREAT BARRIER REEF

About half the size of Texas, Australia's Great Barrier Reef is the only living thing on Earth that's visible from space! The reef was built by colonies of coral that settled on the sea floor and grew to include more than 2,500 reefs in different shapes and sizes. Thousands of kinds of fish and shellfish and 30 kinds of whales and dolphins swim in water that is bathtub-warm all year long—a comfy 70°F to 100°F (21°C to 38°C). Who's ready to jump in?

How grand is the Grand Canyon? Formed about 5 million to 8 million years ago, it's 1 mile (0.6 km) deep and wide enough for the entire state of Rhode Island to fit inside! Rattlesnakes, mountain lions, and black bears live there, but they generally keep to themselves.

GRAND CANYON

MOUNT EVEREST

The tallest mountain is on every serious climber's bucket list. To ascend Mount Everest, climbers need lots of preparation and training. Local guides called sherpas help climbers and carry gear, too. Subfreezing temperatures and hurricane-force winds allow just enough time to take in the view from the summit and snap a selfie. Pack toilet paper and a pee bottle—no bathrooms on the top!

VICTORIA FALLS

Whoosh! Victoria Falls, on the Zambia-Zimbabwe border, isn't the tallest waterfall in the world, but more water rushes down it than at any other. The mist created by the falling water can be seen for miles, and the sound can be heard up to 25 miles (40 km) away. That's more than twice as far as the sound of thunder travels.

PARICUTÍN VOLCANO

Volcanoes have been erupting on Earth for millions of years, making Mexico's Paricutín just a kid. It rose out of a farmer's cornfield in 1943 and continued to grow—and erupt—until 1952. This was the first time that scientists could observe the entire life cycle of a volcano, from birth to extinction. Considered dormant (inactive), it's still a hot spot. When it rains, steam rises from the wide cone.

NORTHERN LIGHTS

In places close enough to the North Pole, the night sky lights up with stunning streaks of color, also called aurora borealis. Though it happens at night, this is caused by the sun, which shoots out tiny particles called electrons that collide with gases in Earth's atmosphere. Auroras closest to Earth are only 60 miles (97 km) away! If you could drive there, the trip would take just an hour on a space superhighway.

THAT'S EXTREME!

HOT AND BUBBLY

Northwest Eifuku sits nearly a mile (about 1.5 km) below the ocean's surface in the Philippine Sea. Bubbling up through its volcanic chimneys is a substance that consists mainly of liquid carbon dioxide at 217˚F (103˚C). That's hotter than boiling water in a kitchen kettle and sounds too toasty for comfort, but some shrimp, fish, CRABS, and mussels call it home.

IT TAKES TWO

The BAT PITCHER PLANT (*Nepenthes hemsleyana*) is native to Borneo, an island in Southeast Asia. It has an unusual way of getting the nitrogen it needs for food. The large upper section attracts bats, which use it as a sound amplifier. While bats send out echolocation calls, using reflected sound (echoes) to locate nearby objects, they leave a nitrogen-rich deposit of guano (poop), which helps the plant grow. Though it might sound gross, this is how two different species help one another.

HORROR-BLE!

BLEEDING TOOTH FUNGUS (*Hydnellum peckii*) may look like a horror movie special effect, but there's nothing fake about it. When water in the ground pushes into the mushroom's roots, it creates a pump-like action that forces it up the stem. When the liquid meets up with a red pigment in the fungus, it created a sap-like goo that oozes out through pores on the top. These fearsome fungi grow in forested areas in North America, Europe, Iran, and South Korea.

COLD AND DEEP

Studying ice, which covers 10% of Earth's surface, is like reading a history book . . . but much colder! Scientists drill down to extract samples called ice cores. The deeper the drilling, the older the ice. **DIFFERENT LAYERS, SUCH AS BLACK VOLCANIC ASH,** reveal secrets about past climate activities that help scientists make predictions about the planet's future.

PEE-YEW

There's no question about it—New Zealand's Wai-O-Tapu geothermal area is a place where heat inside Earth comes out as shooting geysers, bubbling mud pots, and the steaming hot, brilliantly colored **CHAMPAGNE POOL.** The orange and lime green waters are caused by minerals, including sulfur (that's why it smells like rotten eggs). Mud Volcano, at Yellowstone National Park in the United States, is considered the smelliest place in the park.

ROCK SNOT

Yup, that's the common name for **DIDYMO** (*Didymosphenia geminata*), an alga that grows up to 8 inches (20.3 cm) thick in freshwater rivers and streams and clumps onto rocks. It blooms (grows) to cover the water's surface and can suffocate organisms in the water below. Didymo is growing more readily as Earth's waters become warmer. Scientists believe this damaging species is spread by contaminated boots, boats, and equipment that haven't been sanitized before entering a new area.

PUMP ME UP!

MOVE IT! | When you ride a bike to the park, jump rope on the playground, or snowboard down a slope, you're doing aerobic exercise. This increases endurance, so you can play longer without getting tired. The other major kind of exercise is called anaerobic, and it includes lifting weights, sprinting over short distances, and doing the "up" exercises: chin-ups, sit-ups, and push-ups. These help build muscles to make you stronger.

Chapter 3

HUMAN BODY

What if there were a machine that had a sensor so powerful, it could detect about 1 trillion different smells? Oh, and it also had a pump that could work more than 2 billion times in a row. And supporting the inner workings of this device was a material stronger than steel. You might say that's one incredible machine. But it's not a machine at all. It's your body!

That sensitive sniffer is your nose, the hard-working pump is your heart, and one pound of the bones in your skeleton is stronger than a pound of steel. How strong? A small piece of your bone could support the weight of several elephants!

Add in all your organs, including your brain—the command center—and the complex systems that keep everything working, and you'll see that the human body is a true marvel.

BODY BASICS

Your body has five basic regions.

Head There are 22 bones in your skull, and only one of them moves—the jawbone.

Neck The upper part of your spine contains seven bones, called the cervical vertebrae.

Torso Your midsection protects inner organs like your heart and lungs. It's also called the trunk: like the trunk of a tree, it supports your upper "branches" (arms, neck, and head).

Arms Your elbow joint connects the three bones in your arm. Bumping it hits a nerve connected to the upper bone, which is called the humerus. (You may know it as the funny bone, but it's no laughing matter. Ouch!) Below it are the ulna and radius bones—and then your wrists and hands.

Legs From the tips of your toes to your flexible hips, your legs support your body and help you get where you're going.

Skeleton Crew

Bones form the framework of your body. They are living tissue that can grow and repair themselves. It generally takes about 6 to 12 weeks for a bone fracture to heal, if it's properly aligned, stabilized (often with a cast), and immobilized to prevent movement.

Let's Grow!

You're taller when you wake up in the morning than when you went to bed. Gravity compresses your spine during the day, so you shrink almost half an inch (1 cm) by bedtime. There's less pressure on your spine when you're asleep, so you start the next day taller again. Phew!

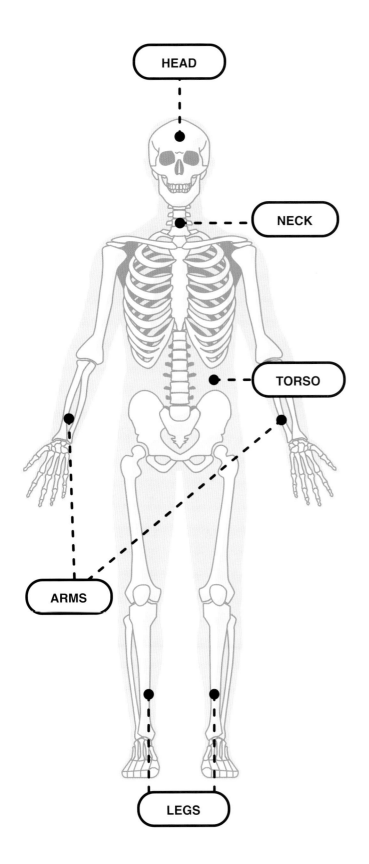

HEAD

NECK

TORSO

ARMS

LEGS

QUIZ

THE SAME OR DIFFERENT?

Check your skeleton savvy with these true-or-false statements.

1. A GIRAFFE'S NECK IS 18 TIMES LONGER THAN A HUMAN BEING'S NECK, SO IT HAS 18 TIMES AS MANY BONES IN IT.

2. YOU HAVE 206 BONES IN YOUR BODY—THE SAME NUMBER YOU WERE BORN WITH.

3. YOU HAVE MORE BONES IN YOUR HANDS THAN IN YOUR FEET.

4. THE SMALLEST BONE IN YOUR BODY IS IN YOUR PINKIE FINGER.

Answers are on page 156.

SURVIVING AND THRIVING

The brain is your command center. This supercomputer receives information from all parts of your body, processes it, and sends out instructions at every moment, even while you are sleeping. Its complex communication system works using chemical and electrical signals that are carried throughout the body. These signals tell your brain what's going on, from the tips of your toes to top of your head, and everywhere in between. How does this amazing organ do so much? It has individual parts that control specific processes and behaviors, all in perfect coordination.

Your Brain at Work

Cerebral Cortex The wrinkled folds of the brain's outer layer give it more surface area for nerve cells to process information than if it were smooth. It is divided into four distinct parts.

- **Frontal Lobe** This is where executive functions like thinking and problem-solving take place. Decision-making, speech production and writing, and your sense of smell are processed here.

- **Parietal Lobe** Physical sensations, such as touch and pain, are processed here. This is also your navigational center—how you figure out where you are relative to objects around you.

- **Temporal Lobe** In addition to forming memories and recognizing objects, this is where you interpret and understand speech.

- **Occipital Lobe** Responsible for vision, this lobe is where your sight is processed.

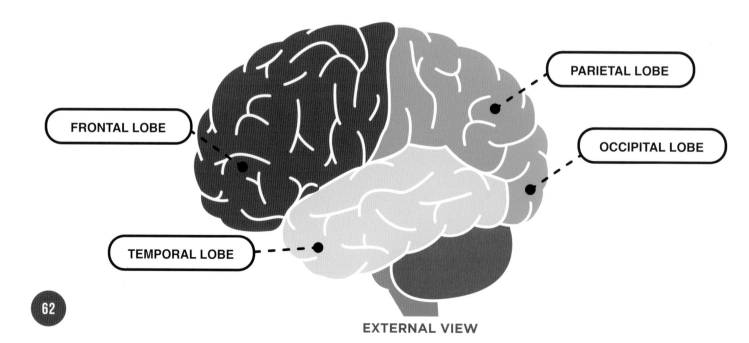

FRONTAL LOBE

PARIETAL LOBE

OCCIPITAL LOBE

TEMPORAL LOBE

EXTERNAL VIEW

Cerebellum This part controls balance and movement; and coordinates muscle groups (motor control) and eye movement. It makes repeated coordinated movements—like riding a bike—possible.

Brainstem Involuntary actions like breathing, swallowing, and your heartbeat are controlled by this area.

Thalamus This is where signals from the sight, hearing, taste, and touch organs are processed, and where your ability to remain alert and focused is controlled. This area also helps you process and regulate your emotions.

Hypothalamus This part keeps all the functions of your body stable. It sends out signals about what your body needs—like sleep, food, and water—and it regulates your body temperature and helps you manage your moods.

Basal Ganglia These groups of neurons specialize in fine-tuning your brain's responses to input, from coordinating body movements and decision-making to the ability to react successfully to a new, unfamiliar situation or experience.

WHAT DOES A NEURON DO ON ITS BIRTHDAY? IT CELL-EBRATES!

DIY

RISE AND SHINE!

Starting your day with breakfast can power your brain, energize your body, and put you in a good mood. Try a yogurt parfait!

In a jar or bowl, spoon ¼ cup vanilla yogurt. Top with granola and fruit, such as berries, and repeat with another layer.

That's good fuel for school!

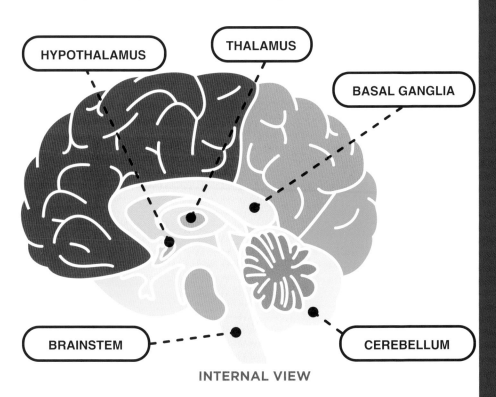

HYPOTHALAMUS

THALAMUS

BASAL GANGLIA

BRAINSTEM

CEREBELLUM

INTERNAL VIEW

GETTING ORGANIZED

An organ is made up of tissues that work together to perform a specific task. Your body has 79 organs. Some of them, like your appendix and tonsils, you can live without. Others, like your brain and those shown here, are vital organs, which means they are essential for survival.

LUNGS

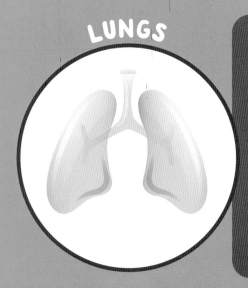

When you breathe in, your lungs fill with oxygen and other gases in the air. Special cells extract the oxygen from the air, and it enters your bloodstream, which carries the oxygen throughout your body, delivering it to all your cells. At the same time, your blood picks up waste gas (carbon dioxide) from your cells and brings it to your lungs, where you exhale it. This cycle is called the gas exchange, and it happens whenever you breathe—about 20,000 times a day!

SKIN

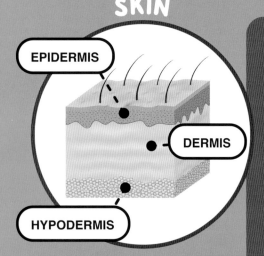

EPIDERMIS

DERMIS

HYPODERMIS

This largest organ makes up about 15% of your body's weight. It has three layers: the epidermis on top, then the dermis, and below that the hypodermis. Your skin helps protect you from extreme temperatures, chemicals, and harmful viruses and germs.

The epidermis sheds dead skin cells all the time. In fact, you get a whole new outer layer about once a month. Other animals shed skin cells, too; dogs and cats get a new epidermis about every three weeks.

LOL! LAUGHTER IS GOOD MEDICINE! IT RELAXES YOUR BLOOD VESSELS, SO YOUR HEART DOESN'T HAVE TO WORK AS HARD.

HEART

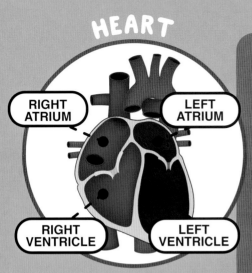

RIGHT ATRIUM

LEFT ATRIUM

RIGHT VENTRICLE

LEFT VENTRICLE

A little larger than an adult's fist, your heart has four chambers. The bottom two, called ventricles, pump blood out to your arteries (blood vessels that take blood from the heart). The top two, called atria, receive blood back from the rest of your body through the veins (blood vessels that bring blood to the heart). Your heart beats about 100,000 times a day, sending out oxygen and nutrients that fuel your body.

KIDNEYS

As your blood circulates through your body, your kidneys clean it. They filter and collect the waste from about 200 quarts (191 l) of blood every day, sending the cleaned blood back to your heart. The waste leaves your body as urine. A person can pee out about 2 quarts (1.9 l) of fluid every day. This would fill up more than 10 bathtubs in a year!

LIVER

Your largest vital organ is about the size of a football. It works like a processing center with hundreds of duties, including regulating chemicals in your blood and creating nutrients. The liver stores vitamins, sends glucose to your brain for it to use as energy, and produces bile, a chemical that helps your body digest food.

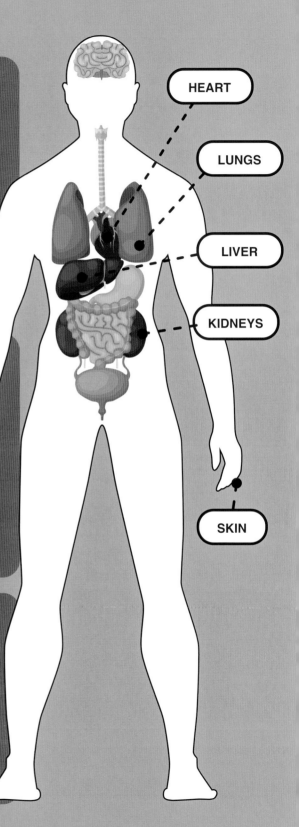

HEART

LUNGS

LIVER

KIDNEYS

SKIN

ALL SYSTEMS GO!

There are 10 major systems in your body. Like athletes on a team, groups of organs work together in each system to perform specific functions.

Integumentary System

Got goosebumps? Your skin is part of a system that includes your glands, hair, nails, and nerves. Some glands enable you to sweat through your pores (small openings in your skin); sweat cools you off when it evaporates on your skin. Other glands produce oil that helps keep your skin healthy and hydrated. Others, around your hair follicles (pores that surround a hair shaft), give you **goosebumps** when you're cold or experience a strong emotion, like fear before going on stage to perform. Your skin also has a built-in repair system to heal cuts and scrapes and knit together new skin.

Hair keeps you warm and protects the top of your head from harmful radiation from the sun. Eyelashes help keep sweat out of your eyes. And nose hairs keep out dust. Here's a hairy fact: the inside of your nose has 100,000 hair follicles—as many as on the top of your head!

GOOSEBUMPS

Muscular System

Muscle fibers are cells that specialize in contracting, because nearly every muscle movement in your body is a form of contraction. Muscles are attached to bones, organs, and blood vessels. Dancers use their muscles to bend, jump, spin, stretch, and stand perfectly still.

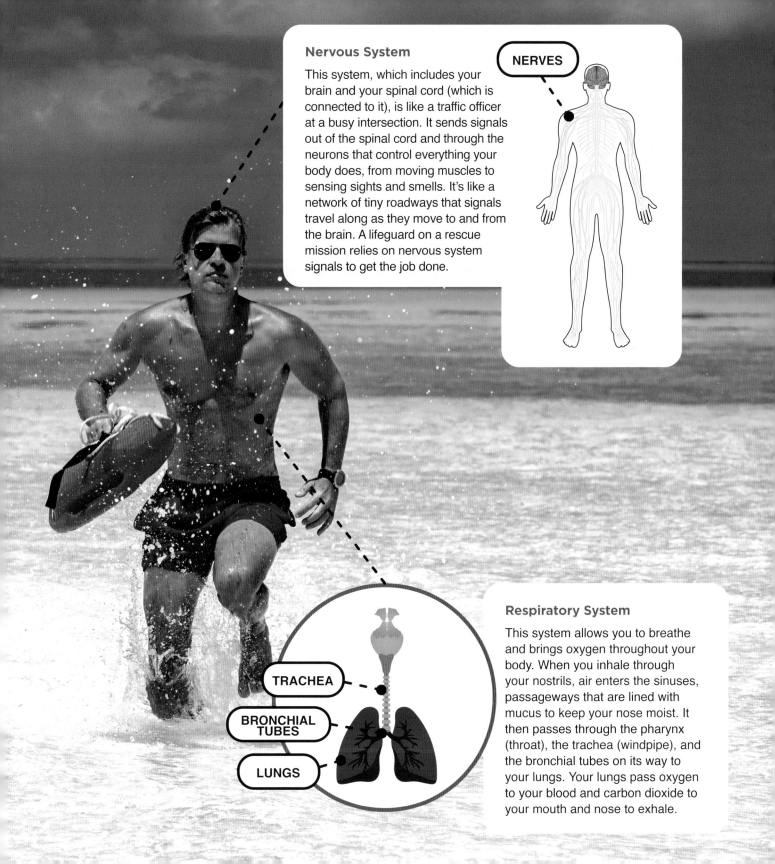

Nervous System

NERVES

This system, which includes your brain and your spinal cord (which is connected to it), is like a traffic officer at a busy intersection. It sends signals out of the spinal cord and through the neurons that control everything your body does, from moving muscles to sensing sights and smells. It's like a network of tiny roadways that signals travel along as they move to and from the brain. A lifeguard on a rescue mission relies on nervous system signals to get the job done.

TRACHEA

BRONCHIAL TUBES

LUNGS

Respiratory System

This system allows you to breathe and brings oxygen throughout your body. When you inhale through your nostrils, air enters the sinuses, passageways that are lined with mucus to keep your nose moist. It then passes through the pharynx (throat), the trachea (windpipe), and the bronchial tubes on its way to your lungs. Your lungs pass oxygen to your blood and carbon dioxide to your mouth and nose to exhale.

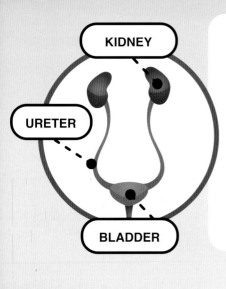

KIDNEY

URETER

BLADDER

Urinary System

This is a cleaning system—it filters out waste from your bloodstream. It's also a drainage system, sending the waste and water (urine) from your kidneys through tubes called ureters on the way to your bladder. The bladder expands like a balloon to hold urine. When it's full, nerves there tell your brain, "Time to let the flow go!" On its way out, urine passes through another tube, called the urethra. Most people need to empty their bladder up to six times a day. Babies pee about twice as often.

Reproductive System

This group of internal and external organs enables people to have babies. The reproductive system develops slowly in humans, with little change from birth to puberty— the tween years when children begin maturing into adults.

Endocrine System

The human body produces more than 50 kinds of hormones—chemical messengers that travel through the body and control various processes. This system is controlled by the brain, and regulates growth, reproduction, emotions, and helps convert food and drink into energy. It kicks off puberty by releasing specific hormones that tell the body what changes to make to help kids grow into adults.

The thyroid gland, found in your neck, is part of the endocrine system. It produces hormones that affect your weight, energy level, temperature, skin, hair and nail growth, and more.

THYROID GLAND

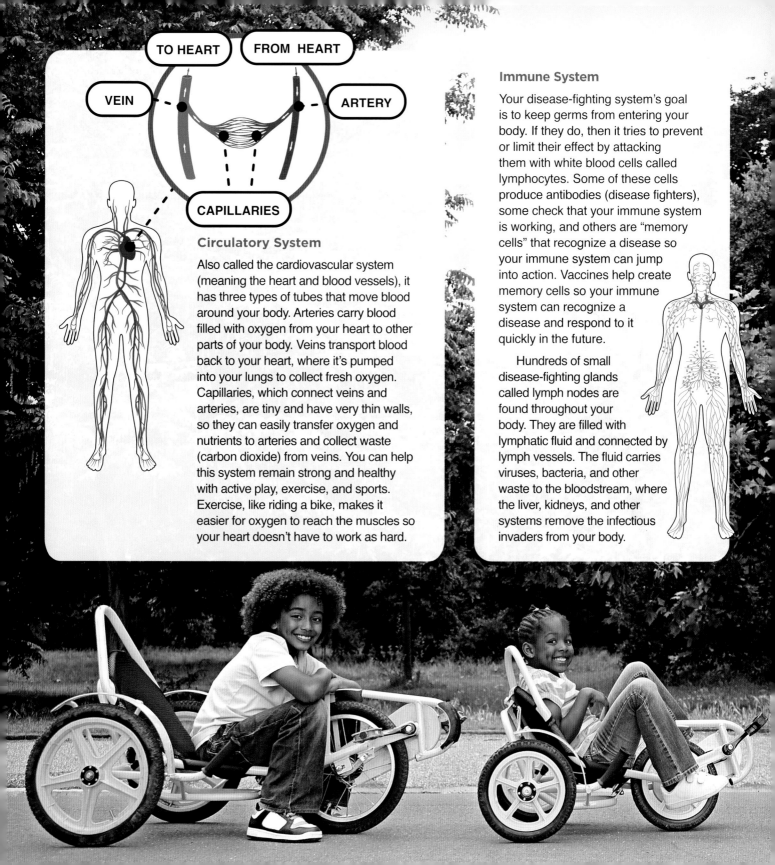

TO HEART **FROM HEART**

VEIN ----- **ARTERY**

CAPILLARIES

Circulatory System

Also called the cardiovascular system (meaning the heart and blood vessels), it has three types of tubes that move blood around your body. Arteries carry blood filled with oxygen from your heart to other parts of your body. Veins transport blood back to your heart, where it's pumped into your lungs to collect fresh oxygen. Capillaries, which connect veins and arteries, are tiny and have very thin walls, so they can easily transfer oxygen and nutrients to arteries and collect waste (carbon dioxide) from veins. You can help this system remain strong and healthy with active play, exercise, and sports. Exercise, like riding a bike, makes it easier for oxygen to reach the muscles so your heart doesn't have to work as hard.

Immune System

Your disease-fighting system's goal is to keep germs from entering your body. If they do, then it tries to prevent or limit their effect by attacking them with white blood cells called lymphocytes. Some of these cells produce antibodies (disease fighters), some check that your immune system is working, and others are "memory cells" that recognize a disease so your immune system can jump into action. Vaccines help create memory cells so your immune system can recognize a disease and respond to it quickly in the future.

Hundreds of small disease-fighting glands called lymph nodes are found throughout your body. They are filled with lymphatic fluid and connected by lymph vessels. The fluid carries viruses, bacteria, and other waste to the bloodstream, where the liver, kidneys, and other systems remove the infectious invaders from your body.

DIGESTION PROGRESSION

What goes in must come out, and that's a job for the digestive system. It extracts nutrients, minerals, vitamins, and water from what you eat and sends the rest on its way out of your body as waste. Here's how it works, intake to output.

1. When you grab a bite of food and start chewing, you produce saliva (spit). This moistens the food in your mouth and helps it enter your gastrointestinal (GI) tract. Saliva contains enzymes—chemicals that break down food, getting the digestion process started.

2. Food moves down a tube called the esophagus and into your stomach. Enzymes and powerful acids in the stomach break down the food into small bits, creating digestive juices.

3. The juices then enter your small intestine. This twisty tube is about 1 inch (2.5 cm) wide and 22 feet (6.7 m) long—that's about as long as four bicycles placed end to end. Here, digestive juices like bile from the gallbladder mix with enzymes from the liver and another organ called the pancreas. The small intestine extracts the nutrients from this mixture and passes them into the bloodstream. What's left over is waste, and most of it moves along into the large intestine.

4. The large intestine is three times wider and about one-fourth as long as the small intestine. Like a processing center, the large intestine reabsorbs water and salt for the body to use and turns the rest of the waste into a soft solid called stool. This takes up to 36 hours to reach the final stop on the digestion journey, the rectum, where it stays until you poop it out through the anus.

Along the Way Most of your urine progresses through the urinary system, but the digestive system plays a part too. Some liquid waste produced in the intestines enters the bloodstream, which takes it to the kidneys, which turn all the body's liquid waste into urine.

On Autopilot?

The brain controls all your muscles' actions. Some of these are voluntary, which means you choose to do something. Some are involuntary, which means they happen without you thinking about them. Chewing and swallowing food is a voluntary action; the rest of the digestive process is involuntary. Your heart beating and your lungs breathing are also involuntary actions.

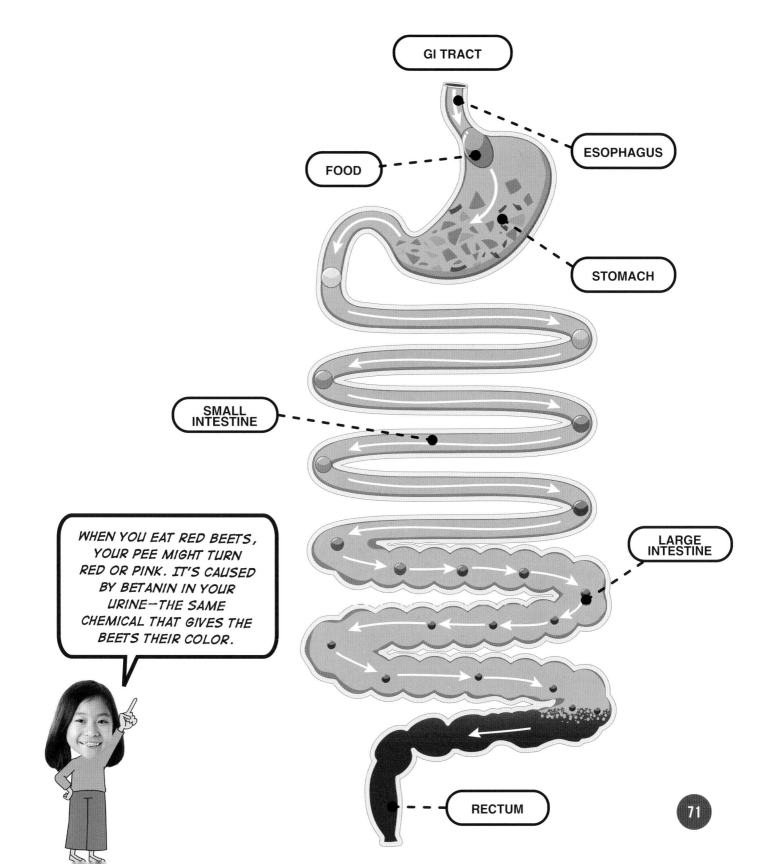

MAKING SENSE OF YOUR SENSES

It seems obvious to say that you see with your eyes, hear with your ears, smell with your nose, taste with your tongue, and feel things with your skin. But what really happens when these sensory body parts pick up signals and send them to your brain?

Hearing The ears work like an audio sound system with a receiver (the eardrum) that vibrates when sound waves enter, an amplifier (three tiny bones called ossicles) that transmits and increases the volume, and electrical signals that carry sound to the brain. Your brain tells you what a sound is, where it's coming from, and how loud, high-pitched, or distant it is.

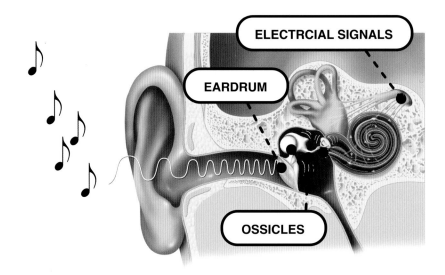

ELECTRCIAL SIGNALS

EARDRUM

OSSICLES

Sight The eyes are like living video cameras that capture light and send it to the brain to be processed. The lens focuses the light and sends it to the retina, which is at the back of the eye. There, nerve cells translate the light into electrical signals that travel along the optic nerve to the brain, which turns this information into images. This happens in as few as 13 milliseconds—about three times faster than an eye blink.

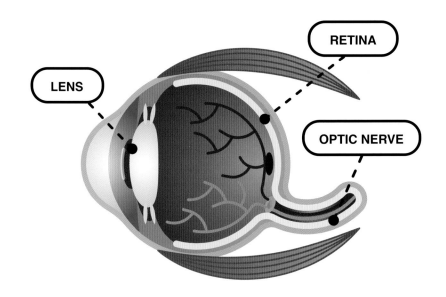

RETINA

LENS

OPTIC NERVE

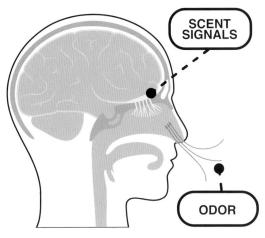

Smell Odor molecules in the air enter your body through your nostrils, where they encounter about 400 scent detectors called receptors. These pass signals to nerves behind the nose that send the information to your brain. While scent sensitivity varies from person to person, scientists think people can recognize up to 1 trillion different odors.

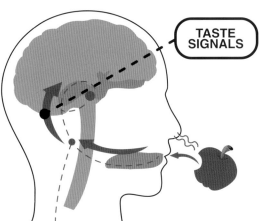

Taste Tiny receptors called taste buds are inside the papillae (bumps) on your tongue. They detect five distinct flavors: salty, sweet, sour, bitter, and savory (also called umami). But taste doesn't stop there. When you chew food, chemicals in the food travel up to your nose. So how things taste involves how they smell, too.

Touch Different neurons in the skin have different sensitivities. Some can distinguish pressure, like a firm handshake. Others can recognize texture, like a soft blanket or a rough washcloth. Some sense pain, some an itch, and some make you ticklish. Just as with the other senses, the information collected through touch is processed in your brain.

WOW!

THE FANTASTIC BRAIN

Some people don't have the use of all five senses. The brain, though, can rewire some neurons and make adjustments. A person without sight might gain sharper hearing or touch.

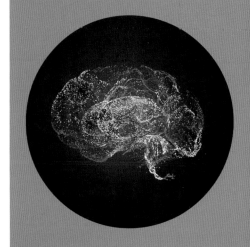

GET A MOVE ON

Like a flashing WALK sign at a street corner, your brain signals your body to start moving. Then a network of bones, muscles, and other body parts starts to work. Most movement involves the places where bones join, such as the ankle, knee, and hip joints.

Your body has three kinds of joints that are made from different materials and work in specialized ways.

Immovable (fibrous) joints don't move. They hold the plates in your skull together to protect your brain. Another kind of immovable joint holds your teeth in your jaws.

Partially movable (cartilaginous) joints are linked by cartilage. These joints move a bit, but not a lot. They give the spine its flexibility, and they're also found in the ribs.

Fully movable (synovial) joints move freely. These are the major joints in the body—hips, shoulders, elbows, knees, wrists, and ankles. These joints are lubricated by synovial fluid so they can move easily.

Within each of these types of joints, there are variations. Examples of fully movable joints include a pivot joint, which allows the head to turn sideways, and a hinge joint, which allows the leg to bend and straighten. The shoulder joint is a ball-and-socket mechanism. The rounded end of the upper arm bone (ball) fits into a concave area of the shoulder (socket).

IMMOVABLE JOINT

PARTIALLY MOVABLE JOINT

FULLY MOVABLE JOINT

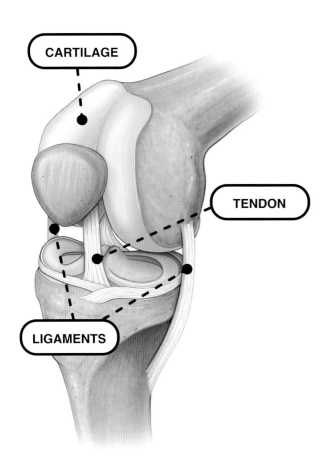

CARTILAGE

TENDON

LIGAMENTS

An Open-and-Shut Case

The knee may look simple, but it is the largest and most complicated joint in the body. It runs from the thigh to the shin, and it involves four bones and two muscle groups. It's a hinge joint, which means it moves back and forth, the way a hinge lets a door open and close. Let's take a peek inside.

Joints rely on **tendons**, which attach muscles to bones, and **ligaments**, which attach bone to bone and support joints. They have other jobs, too. A cordlike tendon helps the eyeball work its muscles. And ligaments hold organs in place, including the stomach, liver, and intestines.

Cartilage acts like a shock absorber in joints, where it absorbs force from movement, and between the ribs and vertebrae in the spine. This sturdy tissue makes up other body parts, too, including your ears and nose.

WOW!

JOINT ENDEAVOR

You are able to walk upright on two feet because your knee joints are strong and can lock. Chimps can stand upright for short periods only— their knee joints can't support their weight on one leg for long, so they walk with knees bent in a kind of side-to-side rocking motion. To see the difference, try this experiment. First, walk 10 steps the way you normally walk. Then, walk 10 steps with your knees bent. Which way was harder? Research shows that humans use about 75% less energy when walking than chimps do, thanks to our sturdy knees.

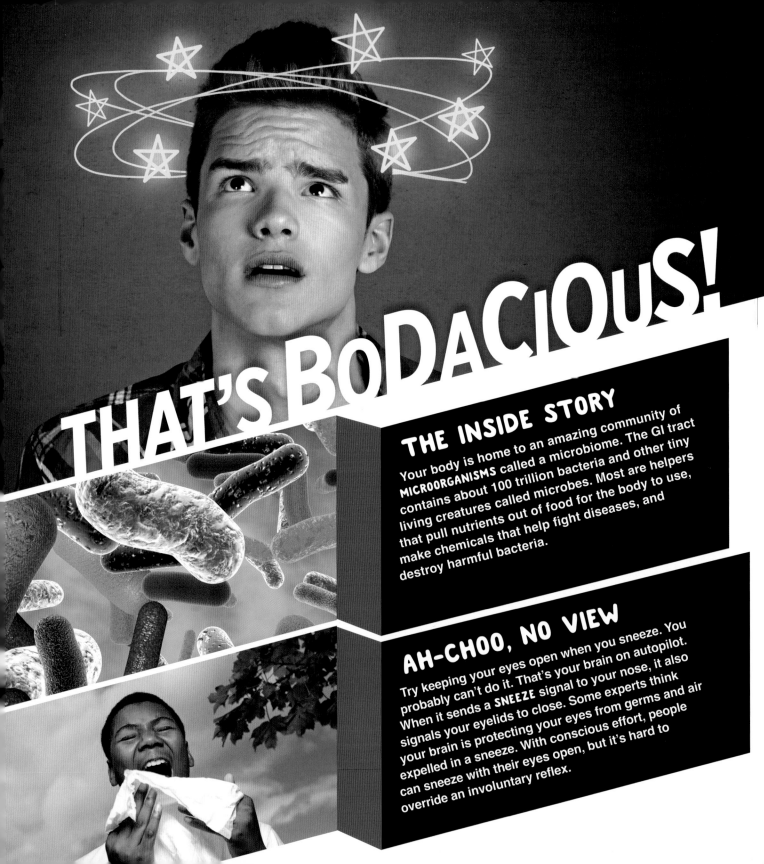

THAT'S BODACIOUS!

THE INSIDE STORY

Your body is home to an amazing community of MICROORGANISMS called a microbiome. The GI tract contains about 100 trillion bacteria and other tiny living creatures called microbes. Most are helpers that pull nutrients out of food for the body to use, make chemicals that help fight diseases, and destroy harmful bacteria.

AH-CHOO, NO VIEW

Try keeping your eyes open when you sneeze. You probably can't do it. That's your brain on autopilot. When it sends a SNEEZE signal to your nose, it also signals your eyelids to close. Some experts think your brain is protecting your eyes from germs and air expelled in a sneeze. With conscious effort, people can sneeze with their eyes open, but it's hard to override an involuntary reflex.

SEEING THINGS

Ouch! Have you wondered if people really see stars when they bump their head? A hard knock to the noggin can cause some neurons in the brain's vision center to fire off. Since not all the visual neurons are affected, the brain doesn't turn the signals into a complete image—it just sees **STARLIKE FLASHES OF LIGHT.**

CATCH!

Have you ever "caught" a yawn by watching someone else's? It's not just humans who **SPREAD YAWNS—** chimps and dogs do too. Why we yawn is still a mystery. Some scientists think it helps cool down the brain or that it brings more oxygen into the blood.

BREAK IT DOWN

The digestive juices in your stomach include hydrochloric acid, a chemical strong enough to dissolve metal. Why doesn't it dissolve you? Your stomach is lined with mucus for protection. When you throw up, the slime factor is **STOMACH MUCUS.** Mucus is also produced in other areas of your body, including your nose and sinuses and in your lungs.

IN THE PINK

Blushing is an involuntary response during which the blood vessels and capillaries under your facial skin get bigger. It happens most often when people feel embarrassed—such as accidentally saying the wrong thing. Experts think that the **PINK-RED TINT** to the cheeks is a way to let others know that you didn't mean any harm. But humans aren't the only species that blushes. Blue-and-gold macaws get pink-cheeked when they're happy or excited.

WHEN THE TEMPERATURE IS ABOVE 32°F (0°C), ICICLES—AND SNOWPEOPLE—MELT.

CHILLIN' | Matter can be liquid, solid, or gas, and it can change from one form to another. An icicle melts on a sunny day, changing from solid ice to liquid water. Heat from the sun can change the water to a gas through evaporation.

Chapter 4

SCIENCE OF MATTER

A rock in your backyard, a river flowing through your town, the air you breathe—those things may not seem to have much in common. But all three—along with all the solids, liquids, and gases that make up Earth—are forms of matter. Matter is any substance that takes up space and has mass. (Mass is a measure of the amount of matter an object contains.)

Matter is all around us—and in us, too! What are its physical and chemical characteristics and how can we recognize them? How does matter change when outside forces—like heat or water—act on it? Let's delve into matters of matter.

WHAT'S THE MATTER?

All matter has physical properties we can observe or measure, like color, size, shape, and weight. For example, a marshmallow is white (usually), round around the middle, with a flat top and bottom. You can feel how heavy it is and tell if it's hard or squishy when you gently press on it. These physical characteristics don't change while you observe them. When heated, the marshmallow is just undergoing a phase transition (from solid to melty liquid), but it retains its chemical properties. Let's look at other physical properties of matter.

Mass is the amount of matter something contains. An object's mass is fixed, which means it never changes.

Weight How much an object weighs depends on the pull of gravity. Someone who weighs 100 pounds (43 kg) on Earth would weigh just 16.5 pounds (7.5 kg) on the moon because of its weaker gravitational pull. Their mass is the same on the moon and Earth.

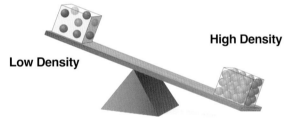

100 lbs (45.4 kg)	16.5 lbs (7.5 kg)
EARTH	MOON

Density is how much of a certain matter is contained in a certain space. If the molecules or atoms in an object are more tightly packed together, it has high density. A plastic spoon has low density and floats in water. But a piece of steel, like a metal spoon, is denser than water and sinks. So how does a big steel cruise ship stay afloat in the ocean? It is filled mostly with air, which is less dense than water.

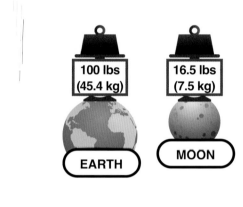

High Density

Low Density

Melting point is the temperature at which solid matter changes to a liquid. When you drop a marshmallow into a cup of hot cocoa, it floats (it's less dense than the hot cocoa). It also melts. In fact, it has a melting point so close to your body temperature that it can start to melt and get sticky in your warm hands.

Boiling point is the temperature at which liquid matter turns into a vapor. Some substances, like nitrogen, boil at very cold temperatures—well below the freezing point of water. Water boils at 212°F (100°C). Some metals, like gold, boil at more than 5,000°F (2,760°C). Yup! Solid metals can even be transformed into gases at high enough temperatures and are found in the atmosphere around some ultra-hot planetary objects..

CHEMISTRY SET

Unlike the physical properties of matter, chemical properties aren't immediately observable. They can be seen only when a substance undergoes a chemical change or reaction. Most of the time, these changes can't be reversed. Studying chemical properties helps us understand things like how toxic (poisonous) a substance is, if it is acidic (sour), and how likely it is to burst into flames. Here are some chemical properties in action.

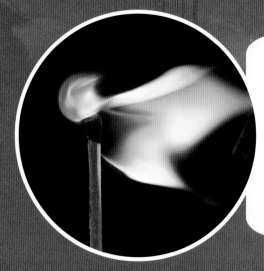

Flammability and Combustion How quickly a substance catches fire, how fast it burns, and the amount of heat it produces are characteristics of flammability. Combustion is a chemical reaction involving fuel (like wood or gas), oxygen, and heat, which work together to create flames. Combustion also creates new chemical substances, such as exhaust from a car engine or soot from a fire.

A motorcycle roars down the road thanks to combustion. Inside the engine's combustion chamber, small amounts of fuel and oxygen mix and are ignited by a spark. That explosion generates enough energy to get the various parts of the engine moving and the bike heading down the road.

Acids and Bases Water-based liquids can be acidic or basic. Acids tend to be sour, like the citric acid in lemon juice and the gastric juices that digest food in your stomach. Bases can feel slippery, like soap and laundry detergent.

A short walk to the school cafeteria is all you need to explore the role acids and bases play in our daily lives. Lactic acid bacteria are added to milk to change the flavor and texture and turn it into cheese. Citric acid occurs naturally in fruits like oranges and grapefruits. And acetic acid is most commonly found in vinegar, which is used to make mustard, ketchup, and pickles. Basic foods tend to taste bitter, like kale and some other leafy greens.

ACIDS   BASES

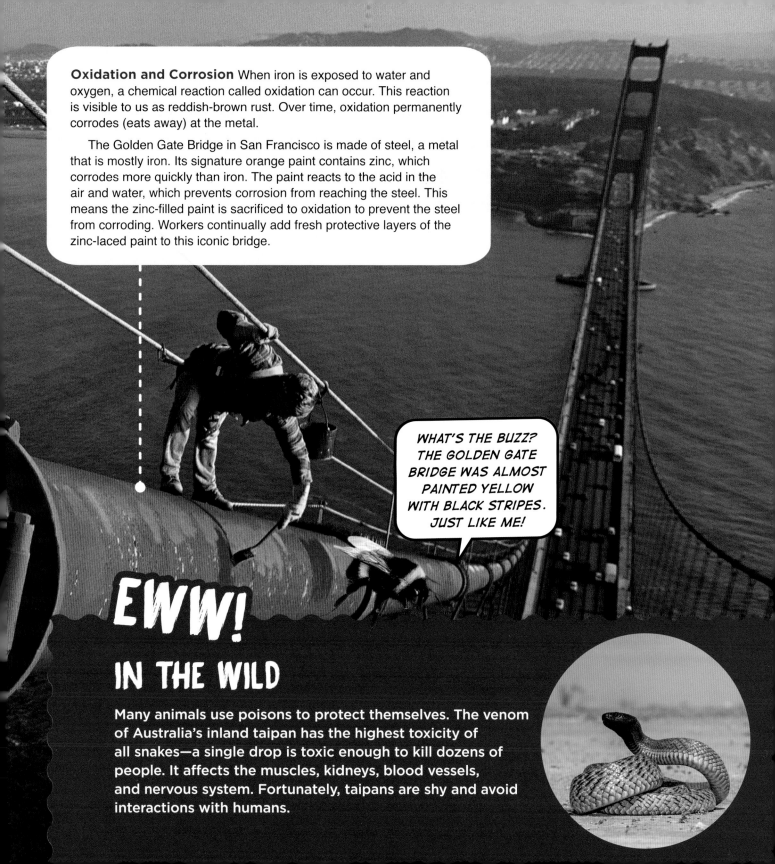

Oxidation and Corrosion When iron is exposed to water and oxygen, a chemical reaction called oxidation can occur. This reaction is visible to us as reddish-brown rust. Over time, oxidation permanently corrodes (eats away) at the metal.

The Golden Gate Bridge in San Francisco is made of steel, a metal that is mostly iron. Its signature orange paint contains zinc, which corrodes more quickly than iron. The paint reacts to the acid in the air and water, which prevents corrosion from reaching the steel. This means the zinc-filled paint is sacrificed to oxidation to prevent the steel from corroding. Workers continually add fresh protective layers of the zinc-laced paint to this iconic bridge.

WHAT'S THE BUZZ? THE GOLDEN GATE BRIDGE WAS ALMOST PAINTED YELLOW WITH BLACK STRIPES. JUST LIKE ME!

EWW!
IN THE WILD

Many animals use poisons to protect themselves. The venom of Australia's inland taipan has the highest toxicity of all snakes—a single drop is toxic enough to kill dozens of people. It affects the muscles, kidneys, blood vessels, and nervous system. Fortunately, taipans are shy and avoid interactions with humans.

EVERYDAY CHEMISTRY

A chemical reaction happens when two or more chemicals combine, breaking their existing bonds to form new ones. Some signs that a chemical reaction has occurred include: heat (like a fire) or light (like a glow stick) is emitted; a substance changes color; gas is created; odor is released; or bits of solid material form in a liquid. They may sound dramatic, but chemical reactions are happening all around, all day long. In fact, we couldn't live without them.

Clean! Soap has been around for more than 2,000 years. This household staple takes two ingredients to make—a base and an acid. The base is a chemical compound, and the acid is a fat or oil. When combined, they undergo a chemical reaction called saponification—the base changes the acid into soap. Other ingredients can be added to determine the color, scent, and consistency.

Soured! Bacteria in milk can turn it sour by converting a sugar (lactose) to lactic acid, which has a sour flavor. The milk can also get lumpy, or curdled, and have a stinky odor when bits of protein in the milk clump together. Called fermentation, this chemical reaction can be positive, too. It's what transforms milk into yogurt.

EWW!
THE KITCHEN STINK

Sauerkraut, tofu, and yogurt are fermented. This means microorganisms—yeast and bacteria—have changed how the starting ingredients taste, smell, look, and feel. Fermentation can also result in some strong-smelling eats. **Natto**—made by fermenting soybeans—is a Japanese food that's sticky and stringy like a gooey mac and cheese. If you're not used to the smell, it might remind you of stinky feet. Is the taste worth putting up with the smell? Try it and see!

Boiled! An egg undergoes chemical reactions when it is cooked. The protein molecules in the egg whites clump together and become firmer the longer they're cooked. When overcooked, compounds in the egg can develop a rotten smell.

Toasted! When you pop a slice of bread in the toaster, it smells yummy and changes color. Called the Maillard reaction, after a French chemist, browning food in this way changes the outside particles, altering the texture—crusty!—and improving the flavor.

DIY

SECRET MESSAGES

Try being a chemist (or a secret agent!) and make a batch of invisible ink. All you need is baking soda, water, two cotton swabs, white paper, and purple grape juice.

Combine equal amounts of baking soda and water in a small bowl and stir. This is your ink. Dip a cotton swab in the ink mixture and write a message on the paper. When it dries, the message will disappear.

To make the message visible again, dip a fresh cotton swab in a little grape juice and brush it over your writing. The juice acts as an acid-base indicator, which means it reacts with the baking soda (a base) in the ink. Ta-da, message revealed!

THAT MATTERS!

GHOSTLY LIGHT

This native Australian organism, called a GHOST FUNGUS (*Omphalotus nidiformis*), turns on the lights at night. A chemical reaction similar to other kinds of bioluminescence—such as glow-in-the-dark fireflies—occurs when chemicals in the fungus mix with oxygen, causing it to glow.

GETTING WARMER

Having trouble getting a metal lid off a glass jar? Use physics to get the job done. Run hot water over the lid. The heat will cause both the glass and metal to expand, but the metal conducts more heat than glass does and it will expand more. Called THERMAL EXPANSION, this creates a little space between the jar and the lid, making it easy to twist off.

SKY LIGHTS

FIREWORKS are big, loud, colorful chemical reactions. A mixture of charcoal, sulfur, and potassium nitrate starts the process. Then heat from a fuse burns the mixture inside a tube, creating gases that shoot the tube into the sky and then explode. Boom! That's combustion at work. Elements add the colors. White is caused by aluminum, red by the element strontium, blue comes from copper, orange comes from calcium, and yellow comes from sodium.

HAPPY 14 BILLIONTH BIRTHDAY!

You're way older than you think. About 10% of your body is made up of hydrogen, a chemical element that was created when the **BIG BANG** occurred almost 14 billion years ago. Other parts of you have a long history, too. The oxygen, nitrogen, and carbon in you came from stars that formed and then exploded billions of years ago.

LIGHTNING ROUND

A lightning bolt carries energy. It heats the air around it to temperatures up to five times hotter than the surface of the sun, and it carries enough electricity to **EXPLODE A TREE**. Through a chemical reaction, it produces ozone. Ozone has a strong odor that reminds some people of the chlorine smell of swimming pools.

LACE UP!

You may think chemical molecules are small, but a polymer is a macromolecule—a very large one made up of chains of identical molecules bound together. Polymers are strong and flexible, and some are waterproof. You can likely find synthetic (manufactured) polymers in **YOUR SHOES**. The tops may be made of leather (a natural polymer), the laces of cotton (which comes from cellulose, a natural polymer), and the padding and soles may contain a synthetic polymer. That's some fancy footwork!

TRANSFORMATION | Energy can't be created or destroyed; it can only be transferred from one object to another. It comes in different forms: a single bolt of lightning includes electrical, thermal (heat), sound, and light energy. A bolt that hits the ground transfers its energy to the ground.

Chapter 5

ENERGY

When we talk about energy, we usually mean things like the sunlight that plants use to make their food, electricity that keeps the lights on, batteries in phones, and foods like energy bars and power drinks. But scientists describe energy simply as the ability to do work. And work is what happens when a force acts on an object to move it in a particular direction. Let's flip the switch and turn on this powerful area of science.

MOTION COMMOTION

Energy can make objects move or change. It's always present all around us, whether we see it or not. When your dog is curled up at your feet, it has potential or stored energy. If the doorbell rings and the dog hops up to see who's there, your dog's potential energy has become kinetic—the energy of motion. More than 300 years ago Sir Isaac Newton came up with three laws to explain motion.

FIRST LAW OF MOTION

An object at rest stays at rest, and a moving object keeps moving in a straight line and at the same speed, unless an unbalanced force affects it. This is called inertia.

Inertia keeps skaters at the top of the ramp until they shift their weight forward. This is an unbalanced force—the foot on the front of the board exerts more force than the foot at the back, causing the skateboard—and you—to start moving down the ramp. Inertia is also how skaters keep moving down the pipe and up the other side without veering in one direction or another.

SECOND LAW OF MOTION

Acceleration—change of speed of motion—depends on an object's mass and the amount of force applied to it.

Force comes into play when skateboarders start their run. They use force to accelerate as they push off, and the greater the force, the faster they go. They also pump their knees to increase their speed, which propels them up the other side of the ramp. Another factor is mass, and it has an inverse (opposite) relationship to force. That means that, if the same amount of force is used, a smaller and lighter skateboarder will gain more speed than a larger and heavier one.

THIRD LAW OF MOTION

For every action there is an equal and opposite reaction. So when one object exerts a force on another object, the second object has an equal and opposite force on the first.

Action and **reaction** are at work when riders "pop." They shift their weight, putting a foot on the tail (back) of the board and pushing down forcefully. This causes an opposite reaction that sends the skateboard (and rider) airborne. Even riding on a flat sidewalk uses Newton's third law—one foot pushes backward on the sidewalk while the other foot moves forward on the skateboard.

But wait . . .

If the law of inertia means that a moving object keeps going, why doesn't the skateboard keep going, making a journey around the world? It's because another invisible force is at work.

Friction is the resistance created when the surface of one thing (the skateboard) slides over the surface of another thing (the pavement or the air). Friction slows things down and creates heat. This resistance slows down moving vehicles, like cars and skateboards. Friction also helps keep your sneaker bottoms from slipping off the skateboard when you're airborne.

HOMEWORK USES THE FORCE OF THE FINGERS ON A KEYBOARD OR A PENCIL ON PAPER TO GET THE JOB DONE.

91

ELECTRICITY, CIRCUITS, AND CURRENTS

Atoms—the building blocks of the universe—are too tiny to see with the naked eye. They contain still tinier particles: a nucleus that contains neutrons and protons, and electrons that revolve around them. When these busy electrons move between atoms, they create electric current.

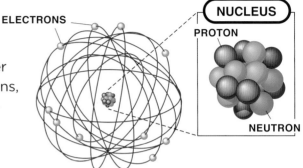

ELECTRONS

NUCLEUS
PROTON
NEUTRON

All Aboard! Any material or object that electricity flows through is called a conductor. Some objects are better conductors than others. Most metals are good conductors, including copper, which is often used in electrical wiring because it lets current flow easily. Electrical wires are encased in rubber or plastic, which acts as an insulator to protect the wires and prevent them from coming in contact with other conductors (which could cause an electric shock or spark a fire).

Follow the Path Electricity travels along a pathway called a circuit, which has a source of power, wires, a switch to turn the flow on and off, and an object that is powered by the current, such as a toaster or a phone charger. The current needs a closed circuit, meaning there is no interruption along the path.

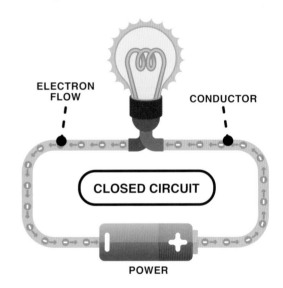

ELECTRON FLOW

CONDUCTOR

CLOSED CIRCUIT

POWER

Energy to Go Electricity has an amazing delivery system! From a power plant, wind, or solar farm, it passes through transformers, which increase the voltage so it can travel long distances through high-voltage transmission lines. The voltage is lowered at a substation, then travels to smaller transformers in your neighborhood. Wires bring it into your house or apartment building, which has its own mini power station—an electrical panel where fuses or circuit breakers control the amount of electricity going through wires in the walls. It then travels to light switches and outlets.

The War of the Currents

There are two types of electrical current. In direct current (DC), the electrons move in only one direction. With alternating current (AC), the electrons move first in one direction and then the other. The use of both types of current was common in the United States until about 150 years ago, when one type won out over the other at the 1893 Chicago World's Fair, shown above.

In the 1870s, scientist and inventor Thomas Edison developed DC current, which was used in the early days of electricity. At about the same time, scientist Nikola Tesla promoted AC current, believing it was superior because it could more easily be adjusted to higher or lower voltages (voltage is the force that creates electrical currents). Tesla invented the first AC system (made up of motors, generators, and transformers). In 1893, the Westinghouse Electric Company, which built and sold electrical systems, chose Tesla's AC current to power the Chicago World's Fair. Soon after, General Electric, which had acquired Edison General Electric Company just five years before the fair, switched from using DC to AC current and the war was won, making AC the dominant current. *Sort of.* Today, computers, batteries, solar cells, and electric vehicles use DC power.

QUIZ

A SHOCKING QUIZ

Can you tell these electric facts from fiction? Test your knowledge with these true-or-false statements.

1. ELECTRICITY TRAVELS MUCH FASTER THAN LIGHT.

2. ELECTRICITY IN YOUR BODY MAKES YOUR HEART PUMP.

3. INSTEAD OF EYESIGHT, SOME EELS RELY ON ELECTRIC CHARGES TO HUNT FOR FOOD.

4. AN ELECTRIC POPCORN POPPER WAS INVENTED WAY BACK IN 1905.

For answers, see page 156.

SOUND AND LIGHT

Waves are a form of energy with a repeating pattern called a cycle. They can be tall or shallow and more or less frequent. Sound and light travel from one place to another in waves.

Hear This

Sound waves come from vibrations that can travel through air, water, and even solid objects. When those waves reach you, they make parts of your ear vibrate, and your brain recognizes these vibrations. This is why you can hear a loud stereo in a nearby car, even when the windows are closed.

That Hertz

The speed at which a sound wave travels is its frequency, and the greater the frequency, the higher the pitch. Frequency is measured in hertz (Hz), which is the number of wave cycles per second. Human ears typically hear sounds between 20 and 20,000 Hz.

Below 20 Hz	Elephants use this range for vocal rumbles, which travel over several miles (km), helping them communicate with their herd. This frequency is too low for humans to hear.
85 to 250 Hz	Average range of the human voice
250 to 6,000 Hz	Average daily sounds humans hear
400 to 500 Hz	The honk of a car horn
10,000 Hz	**The sound of crashing cymbals**
45,000 Hz	The higher-pitched sound a dog can hear that you can't
120,000 Hz	Ultrasonic sounds bats use to navigate in the dark

WOW!

WAH! WAH!

A baby wails at 300 to 600 Hz, which sounds loud and urgent. A study showed that domestic cats have a similar tactic to get our attention. They use a higher pitched, more urgent meow hidden inside a purr—in the range of a baby's cry and twice as high as a cat's usual sound—when it's time for chow.

Lights On

Light travels in waves, too. Some light is visible, like light bulbs, fireworks, rainbows, and computer screens. But most of the light in our universe is invisible to us. This range of visible and invisible light is called the electromagnetic spectrum.

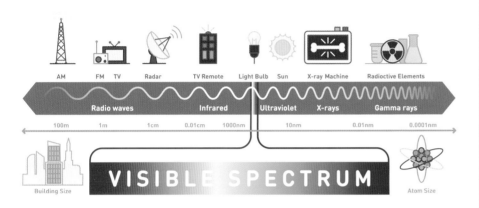

AM	FM TV	Radar	TV Remote	Light Bulb Sun	X-ray Machine	Radioactive Elements

Radio waves | Infrared | Ultraviolet | X-rays | Gamma rays

100m | 1m | 1cm | 0.01cm | 1000nm | 10nm | 0.01nm | 0.0001nm

VISIBLE SPECTRUM

Building Size

Atom Size

Radio waves carry signals to your TV and allow your mobile phone to send signals wirelessly.

Infrared makes the remote control work with a beam of energy, and it also makes objects easier to see in the dark with night vision goggles.

Ultraviolet can disinfect surfaces, can reduce the spread of bacteria, and can harden materials like dental fillings. It occurs naturally as part of sunlight.

X-rays help your dentist see if you have cavities or cracks in your teeth. They can pass through skin and organs, but not through teeth or bones.

Gamma rays have the most energy. They are produced by lightning and stars.

HOW DID ONE LIGHT GREET ANOTHER? IT WAVED!

THAT'S RENEWABLE!

SOLAR STUNNER

Light from the sun is collected using technology that turns sunlight into electricity using photovoltaic (PV) cells. Also called solar cells, they can be as thin as four human hairs and are grouped together on large panels that contain from 32 to 144 PV cells. The **LARGEST SOLAR FARM IN THE UNITED STATES** is located in California. Its 9 million solar panels power 180,000 homes. At 9.5 square miles (25.6 sq km), this solar farm is as big as 4,600 football fields and can be seen from space!

DATA COLLECTOR

OCEAN RESEARCH BUOYS don't need a lot of power, but getting it to them is challenging. Outfitted to run on solar or wave energy, an ocean weather research buoy can get the energy it needs from nature to measure and record data on sea surface temperature, air temperature, wave height, storm surge, wind speed, and rainfall, along with the effects of hurricanes and tsunamis.

WIND WIND-UP

GIANT TURBINES with propeller-like blades that can be as long as 18 school buses in a row convert the wind's kinetic energy into mechanical energy as the blades spin. This energy is converted to electrical energy by a generator inside the turbine, and it travels through underground cables to the power grid (a vast network that delivers electricity to consumers).

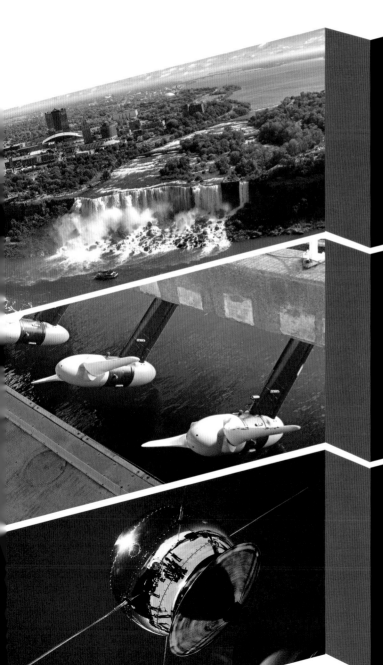

HYDROPOWER

Water flows from higher to lower ground, and dams convert moving water in rivers and streams to electricity. This is an example of potential energy becoming kinetic energy. The water is collected in a holding area called a reservoir, then released in a controlled way to flow past turbines connected to a generator. Power stations on the **NIAGARA RIVER** generate 25% of the power used in New York State and Ontario, Canada.

TURNING TIDES

A **TIDAL TURBINE** is similar to a wind turbine, but it works in the ocean. The movement of tides going out and coming in, along with ocean waves and currents, turn turbine blades to generate electricity. Water is about 800 times denser than air, so tidal turbines need to be heavier and sturdier than wind turbines.

THE O.G.s

Renewable energy—which comes from sources that won't run out, like the sun, wind, and water—isn't as new as it may seem. **VANGUARD 1**, the first solar-powered satellite, was launched into space by the United States in 1958. The size of a small melon, it's still in orbit today. And wind power has been around for thousands of years. Before humans learned how to generate electricity, windmills were used to grind grain, pump water, and power machinery in sawmills to cut wood.

MORE THAN 1,000 DINOSAUR TRACKS HAVE BEEN FOUND HERE!

SURF'S UP! | Catch The Wave at Vermilion Cliffs National Monument in northern Arizona and travel back to a time and place where dinosaurs stomped and roamed. Over millions of years, sand dunes in this former desert compacted and hardened into rock. Rain carved deep canyons and wind erosion shaped the peaks.

Chapter 6

EARTH

Our planet has been around for about 4.5 billion years. It began as space dust and gases that clumped together with the help of gravity, and was shaped by many forces, both below and above its surface.

The earliest evidence of life on Earth—microscopic organisms called microbes—dates back about 3.5 billion years. Over time, different life forms appeared and then evolved as they spread across the planet. Today, Earth is home to about 8 billion people, 400,000 kinds of plants, and more than 1.6 million known species of animals. Based on evidence discovered so far, Earth is the only planet in our solar system that has life. Read on to learn more about our planet.

WHAT IS EARTH MADE OF?

From the Inside Out

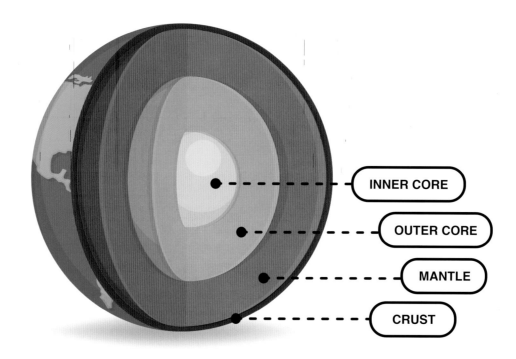

INNER CORE

OUTER CORE

MANTLE

CRUST

Inner Core Earth's center is a solid ball about 759 miles (1,221 km) thick. If you could ride a bike through the core, it would take more than 90 hours. It is made of iron, nickel, and other metals, including gold. It's super hot—up to 9,800°F (5,400°C). That's about as hot as the sun's surface!

Outer Core Twice as thick as the inner core at 1,500 miles (2,400 km), this liquid layer floats above and around the inner core. It is made up mostly of nickel and iron.

Mantle This layer starts about 18 miles (30 km) below Earth's surface and is 1,800 miles (2,900 km) thick. It's mostly solid rock, but the movement of some rock masses above the liquid outer core shaped our planet and still causes events like earthquakes and volcanoes.

Crust Right under your feet is Earth's crust. Beneath the ocean, the crust is about 3 miles (5 km) thick. The crust under land areas can be up to 43 miles (70 km) thick.

The Air Up There

You can't see the atmosphere, but it's all around us, providing the air we breathe and protecting us from most of the sun's ultraviolet (UV) radiation. It's made of many layers and they all have different jobs.

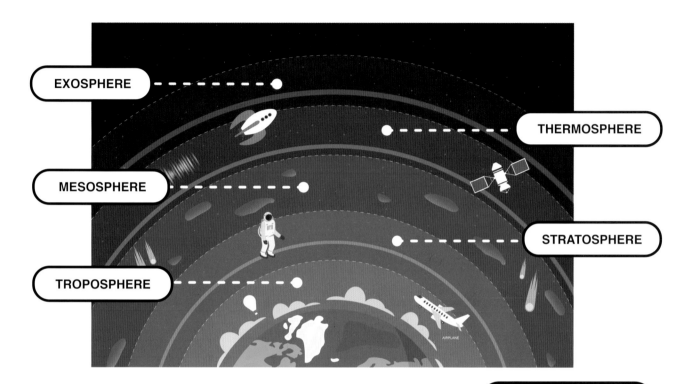

Troposphere This layer contains the air we breathe and keeps Earth's temperature livable. It's also where our weather forms. It gets cooler the higher you go.

Stratosphere The stratosphere absorbs most of the sun's harmful UV radiation. Because it's nearly cloudless and weather-free, planes fly in the lower stratosphere to avoid the turbulence of the troposphere.

Mesosphere The mesosphere is extremely cold and acts as a force field to protect Earth. This is where meteors and space rocks burn up before they can land on Earth, appearing as shooting stars in the night sky.

Thermosphere This layer doesn't have any clouds or water vapor, but it's where the auroras (northern and southern lights) form and many satellites orbit.

Exosphere Scientists often disagree about whether this is the outer edge of Earth's atmosphere or the beginning of outer space. It's about 6,200 miles (10,000 km) thick. Satellites, including the International Space Station, can orbit here.

IF YOU COULD FALL THROUGH THE CENTER OF EARTH FROM ANYWHERE IN THE CONTINENTAL U.S., YOU'D END UP IN THE INDIAN OCEAN.

DON'T FORGET TO PACK YOUR SCUBA GEAR!

GET THE DRIFT

About 250 million years ago (MYA), you could travel from North America to Africa without crossing an ocean. That's because all the land on Earth was crammed together into one supercontinent that scientists today call Pangaea. Over millions of years, this supercontinent broke up and the pieces drifted apart. Divided by large bodies of water, they formed the seven continents we have today. The movement of sheets of rock called tectonic plates in Earth's mantle caused this continental drift.

Here's what the continents have looked like over millions of years.

PERMIAN PERIOD

252 MYA

On the supercontinent, most climates were dry and received little rain. Reptiles did well in these conditions, but for reasons scientists haven't yet discovered, they and other species began to die off. By the end of this period, about 95% of all animal species were wiped out. But there are Permian period rocks on all our continents today.

Scutosaurus

TRIASSIC PERIOD

LAURASIA

GONDWANA

200 MYA

During this period, Pangaea spilt into two continents— Gondwana and Laurasia— and the first dinosaurs and mammals began to appear. One early mammal called *Morganucodon* was tiny, weighing just 1 to 3 ounces (27 to 89 gm), had hair-covered skin, and hearing similar to today's rodents.

Morganucodon

JURASSIC PERIOD

150 MYA

Gondwana split into Antarctica, Africa, Australia, South America, and what's called the Indian subcontinent. Laurasia split into North America, Europe, and the rest of Asia. The splitting created new oceans, and some of them flooded the continents. During this period, shallow-water seas covered parts of the western United States. Earth became warmer and more tropical. Dinosaurs flourished, and the first birds took to the skies.

Archaeopteryx

Dakotaraptor

CRETACEOUS PERIOD

66 MYA

During this period, Gondwana's landmasses continued to move apart, forming roughly the continents we know today. Dinosaurs, including the fierce *Tyrannosaurs rex*, stomped around, and oceans brimmed with life, including the first turtles that lived fully in water, and long-necked reptiles called mosasaurs and plesiosaurs. The first flowering plants appeared.

CENOZOIC ERA

TODAY

Our continents continue to drift—very slowly! While it varies from place to place, on average they drift 0.06 inch (1.5 mm) a year. Geoscientists—experts who study Earth to understand its past, present, and future—believe that hundreds of millions of years from now, the continents may crash together again and form a new supercontinent.

QUIZ

DINO DISCOVERY

Test your knowledge of prehistoric particulars with these true-of-false statements.

1. ALL DINOSAURS BECAME EXTINCT.

2. DINOSAURS HAD BRIGHTLY COLORED FEATHERS.

3. *T. REX* AND *STEGOSAURUS* WERE FIERCE FOES.

4. YOU DRINK THE SAME WATER THAT DINOSAURS DRANK.

Answers are on page 157.

Tyrannosaurus rex

Cassowary

IT'S PREHISTORIC

When you encounter a mystery, you look for clues to solve it. Paleontologists are scientists who study fossils, which are the preserved remains of dinosaurs, plants, and other organisms, to solve the mystery of Earth's history. So far, scientists have determined that Earth has had four distinct eras.

A giant asteroid landed in Chicxulub, Mexico, 66 million years ago.

Precambrian Era
4.5 Billion to 541 Million Years Ago

A time of early life, this is when our atmosphere began to form. Soft-bodied creatures like sponges and worms lived in the oceans. The oldest fossils, of a kind of bacteria, were discovered in Western Australia. They're 3.47 billion years old.

Stromatolites were formed by communities of microbes that trapped sediment, building up layer after layer. Living stromatolites can be found today in only a few places, including Australia and the Bahamas.

Paleozoic Era
541 Million to 252 Million Years Ago

Sea creatures from this time included ancestors of today's insects, shellfish, and spiders. Toward the end of this era, fish with spines appeared, and some adapted to living on land.

Trilobites ranged in size from 28 inches (72 cm) to barely bigger than the sharp point of a pencil. Their closest living relative is the horseshoe crab.

Mesozoic Era
252 Million to 66 Million Years Ago

During the age of dinosaurs, there were fierce predators like *Tyrannosaurus rex* and *Giganotosaurus*, and plant-eaters like *Triceratops* and *Apatosaurus*. Some reptiles lived in water, such as mosasaurs, ancient ancestors of snakes and monitor lizards. Pterosaurs, the first fliers, ranged in size from as small as a pigeon to as large as a fighter jet. Early mammals also appeared during this era.

This era ended when a gigantic asteroid crashed into Earth, creating a huge crater, a cloud of dust and gases, and colder temperatures. This wiped out about 75% of all animal species, including the dinosaurs, and more than half the plant species. Cockroaches, crocodiles, and sharks are among the animals that survived.

Water-dwelling reptiles called ichthyosaurs were about 10 feet (3 m) long. Initially, they swam by moving their thin, long bodies from side to side. Over time, these distant relatives of snakes and lizards evolved to speed through the water by tail power alone.

Cenozoic Era
66 Million Years Ago to Today

As Earth recovered from the asteroid crash, more birds appeared. Without the giant dinosaurs thundering around, mammals took center stage. This is when the first primates appeared, along with most of the life forms we know today, including ancestors of today's horses, elephants, camels, dogs, cats, and whales. The earliest human ancestors appeared 5 to 7 million years ago, and the first modern humans, *Homo sapiens*, appeared in Africa about 200,000 to 300,000 years ago.

The giant rhinoceros lived in Asia more than 20 million years ago. Likely the largest land mammal ever, one species was about four times taller than a modern rhino and weighed more than ten times as much!

SCIENTISTS STUDY FOSSILIZED VOMIT TO LEARN WHAT PREHISTORIC ANIMALS ATE.

ROCK ON

A rock may seem like a permanent object, but it's not. It's always in the process of changing, due to natural forces like gravity, heat, and erosion (from wind, water, and human activities). Over millions of years, one type of rock becomes another.

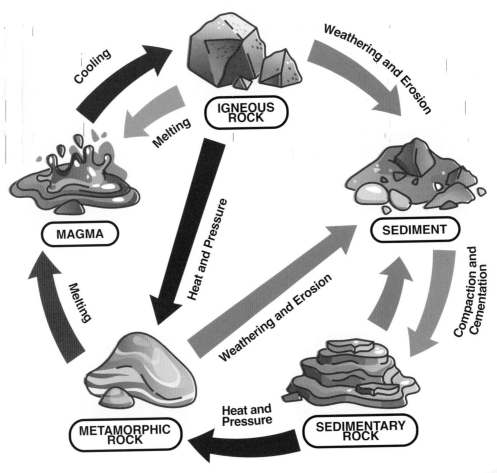

Cooling

Weathering and Erosion

IGNEOUS ROCK

Melting

Heat and Pressure

MAGMA

SEDIMENT

Weathering and Erosion

Compaction and Cementation

Melting

Heat and Pressure

METAMORPHIC ROCK

SEDIMENTARY ROCK

DIY
MAKE A PET ROCK

Paint a rock pet, farm, or zoo. All you need are smooth stones, paint pens or water-based patio or acrylic paint, and brushes.

To get started, give your rock a base coast of a single color and let it dry. That will help your design show up best. Then add eyes, a nose, mouth, ears, hair, or fur—there's no wrong way to paint a rock. Let the rock dry overnight. Have fun and let your creativity run wild!

Rock Solid

There are three types of rocks. They form in different ways and contain different materials. Rocks are strong and durable—they can withstand wear and tear—which makes them excellent materials for buildings and sculptures.

SEDIMENTARY Small particles of larger rocks, minerals, and organic debris—called sediment—are pressed together to form larger rocks. Some common sedimentary rocks include limestone, sandstone, and shale.

The Empire State Building in New York City and the Great Pyramid of Giza in Egypt are both made of limestone, which contains calcium carbonate—the same material in coral reefs.

IGNEOUS These rocks get their start as magma (hot liquid and semi-liquid rock) in Earth's crust and mantle. Magma becomes lava that flows out of volcanoes and hardens into igneous rock as it cools. Common igneous rocks include basalt and granite.

Mount Rushmore in South Dakota is carved from granite. This is the most common igneous rock found on Earth's surface.

METAMORPHIC These are sedimentary or igneous rocks that go through a change called metamorphism when subjected to intense heat and pressure. Metamorphism happens deep underground or where two tectonic plates grind together, creating friction and heat. Common metamorphic rocks include gneiss (NICE) and marble.

The Taj Mahal in India and the Lincoln Memorial in Washington, D.C., and are both made from marble.

DIGGING DEEP

Caves are openings within rocky formations. They come in many sizes and were formed in different ways. They can be narrow passageways or giant rock halls hundreds of miles long. Some were carved out by water; others are tunnels left behind as lava cooled. You can be an armchair speleologist (cave explorer) and take a peek inside some of Earth's most interesting caves.

CAVE OF THE CRYSTALS, MEXICO

The climate in this underground cave is brutal. Temperatures can top 136°F (58°C) and humidity is about 99%, so researchers need to limit visits to short periods of time and wear special clothing to stay cool. It's home to a spectacular sight—the world's largest known crystal. Made from the mineral gypsum, this giant formation weighs up to 55 tons (50 mt)—heavier than a humpback whale!

This is one cool cave—it's the largest ice cave in the world! It has a natural two-way cooling system. In winter, cold air blows in from the outside, refreezing melting snow and ice in the cave. In warmer weather, cold air blows out of the cave, keeping ice near the entrance from melting. This process creates the cave's famous ice "sculptures."

EISRIESENWELT ICE CAVE, AUSTRIA

MAMMOTH CAVE, KENTUCKY

The longest known cave system in the world stretches underground for at least 405 miles (652 km), a little less than the distance from Washington, D.C., to Boston. The cave is famous for its speleothems, formations created by the minerals calcite and gypsum, which are found in water in the cave. Some of the speleothems are called popcorn because that's what they look like.

This cave was first discovered in 1968, and there were more than a dozen expeditions, each going deeper, in an attempt to discover how deep this cave plunged. In 2018, a team of speleologists spent four days making the difficult descent all the way to the bottom, which lies 1.4 miles (2.2 km) down, making this the world's deepest cave.

VERYOVKINA CAVE, ABKHAZIA (GEORGIA)

WAITOMO GLOWWORM CAVES, NEW ZEALAND

The "glowworms" that cling to this cave's ceiling aren't actually worms. They're the larvae of a type of gnat (an insect). They get their glow from chemicals in their bodies that create light to attract prey, which they catch with long strings of sticky mucus.

UNDERGROUND AND ON THE MOVE

Jump in a lake or go tubing in a river and you'll be enjoying some of the 1% of Earth's surface that is fresh water. About two-thirds of Earth's fresh water is stored in glaciers and ice caps, and one-third is underground. This groundwater provides drinking water for more than half the world's population.

What is it and where does it come from? Groundwater occurs naturally and collects in shallow or deep areas called aquifers beneath our feet. And it's recharged (replenished) by precipitation and snowmelt.

The amount of groundwater in any location varies. Too little rain can reduce the amount of available fresh water in an aquifer. So can too much rain; if the ground gets too saturated, then the water forms runoff and doesn't sink into the ground. And if we remove too much water from the ground, aquifers can run dry. In the United States, about 38% of people living in cities rely on groundwater, and in rural communities that number tops 90%. Groundwater helps grow the food we eat, because it is used to irrigate crops. It's also a critical resource for animals and plants; is used by businesses such as clothing and paper manufacturers, mining companies, and power plants; and refills our lakes and rivers.

AQUIFER

WATER MOLECULES STICK TOGETHER SO WELL THEY CAN OVERCOME GRAVITY. NATURAL PRESSURE IN AN AQUIFER CAN CAUSE WATER TO BURST THROUGH THE GROUND WITHOUT THE HELP OF A PUMP.

TASTY TIDBIT More than three-quarters of the land in Kansas is used for growing food for people to eat.

WOW!

BIG GULPS

The largest and deepest aquifer in the world is the **Great Artesian Basin** in Australia. It is 9,800 feet (3,000 m) deep and covers an area about as large as Alaska. The largest aquifer in the United States is the Ogallala Aquifer, which lies beneath parts of eight states: Colorado, Kansas (shown above), Nebraska, New Mexico, Oklahoma, South Dakota, Texas, and Wyoming.

WORLD WATER DAY

MARCH 22

World Water Day

The United Nations established an annual World Water Day to remind everyone to protect this natural resource.

BUBBLING UP

Some underground water erupts through the surface, shooting up in columns of hot water and steam called a geyser. The water can rocket up more than 300 feet (91 m)—as tall as London's Big Ben. Geysers are rare. Only about 1,000 exist around the world, and most appear where volcanoes were once active.

There are two kinds of geysers. Fountain geysers shoot out water in different directions. Cone geysers erupt in a tight stream as the water passes through a cone-shaped collection of minerals.

SAY WHEN? It can be hard to know when a geyser will erupt. Yellowstone National Park's Steamboat Geyser (a cone geyser) once went 50 years without erupting. Then, in 2020, it erupted almost 50 times! But **Old Faithful**, also a cone geyser at Yellowstone, erupts on a fairly regular schedule, which is how it got its name. If you arrive a moment too late to see the spectacular display, you'll only have to wait about 90 minutes for the next one.

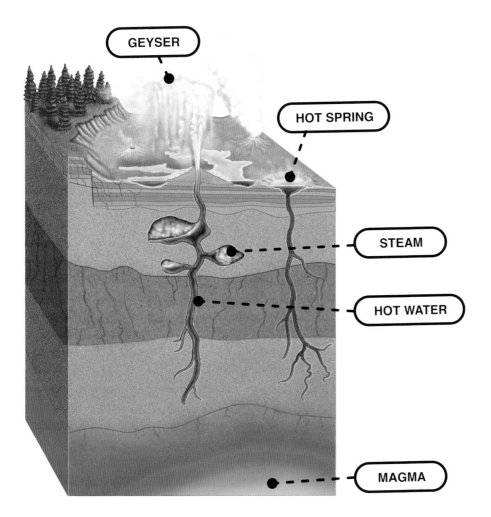

GEYSER

HOT SPRING

STEAM

HOT WATER

MAGMA

Cooking Up a Geyser

Geysers need three ingredients to form: water, magma to heat it, and what's called a plumbing system—a way for the hot water and steam to reach the surface. The rocks underground are strong enough to stay together under the high pressure created by the hot water and steam a geyser produces. But some of the water shoots out of openings in the rock and up into the air. Slowly, the openings refill with hot water, and the process starts again.

The Spring's the Thing

Yellowstone National Park, which is located in Wyoming, Montana, and Idaho, is a hotbed of more than 10,000 hydrothermal features created by underground hot water and steam that has reached the surface. These include more than 500 geysers, bubbling areas called mudpots, steam vents, and hot springs.

Hot springs are places where hot water collects in pools. Tiny organisms called thermophiles thrive in the superheated water. Hot springs often have varying rainbow hues, which form when groups of thermophiles gather by the billions.

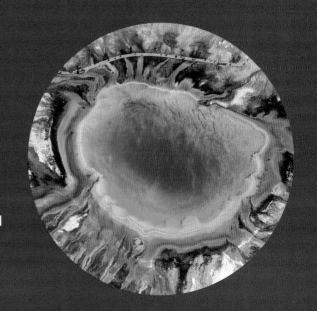

MOTION IN THE OCEAN

About 97% of all surface water is in the planet's five oceans: the Pacific, Atlantic, Indian, Arctic, and Southern. If you look out at an expanse of ocean water or see it down below from an airplane window, it may look quite still. But ocean water is constantly moving—on its surface and deep below. Winds blowing along the surface create waves. Tidal waves come ashore on beaches. And storms, such as hurricanes, create a stir. Other natural forces keep the ocean in motion, too, including the way our planet moves around the sun. The gravitational effects of the sun and moon on Earth move tides from their highest to lowest levels and back again.

Keeping Current

Ocean water moves in currents. These are like rivers of water on and below the ocean's surface. Wind, gravity, water temperature, and the amount of salt in the water create currents. One of the world's most well-known currents is the Gulf Stream. It starts in the Gulf of Mexico and travels east across the Atlantic Ocean, moving much more water each day than in all of Earth's rivers.

Deep ocean currents help shape the climate above the surface. In a kind of circular loop like a conveyer belt, they carry warm water from the equator and cold water from the polar regions. This movement keeps air and water temperatures from overheating in some areas or getting too cold in others.

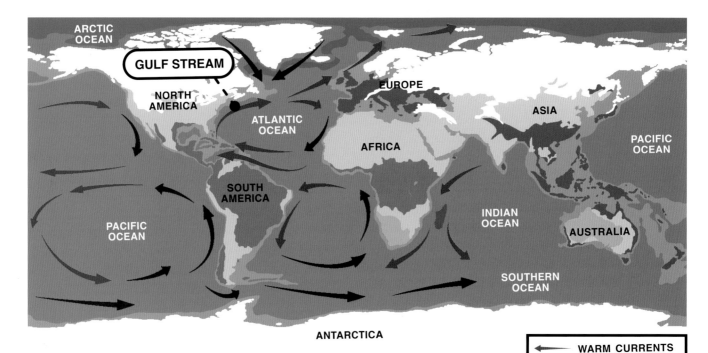

EWW!

Our Changing Climate

Sunshine, rain, and snow are weather—the current conditions where you are. Climate is what the weather is like over a long period of time. Earth's climate is getting warmer, and even an increase of just a few degrees can have a big impact on our planet.

Oceans absorb most of the sun's heat, and as oceans warm, some ocean creatures are forced out of their usual habitats. And in warmer waters, the algae living in coral is expelled, turning the coral white (called coral bleaching). This affects the animals that live and feed around coral reefs, forcing them to look for new homes.

BLEACHED CORAL

A DEEP DIVE The ocean has deep areas called trenches. They're usually found where tectonic plates crash together. The deepest spot on Earth is at the bottom of the Mariana Trench in the western Pacific Ocean, almost 7 miles (11 km) below the ocean surface. It's dark, freezing, and the pressure from the water above is estimated to be more than 1,000 times the pressure at sea level (the top level of the ocean). That crushing force makes it hard for objects to move through the water. **Remotely operated vehicles (ROVs)** can explore some of our deeper waters while being controlled with a video game–like joystick by a driver at the surface.

SHAPING UP

Powerful forces continually shape and reshape Earth's surface. Wind blows sand into dunes and erodes rocks. The movement of tectonic plates forms mountains, and earthquakes (also caused by the movement of tectonic plates) can create landslides.

Weathering and Erosion Australia's **Pinnacles** are one stunning example of the power of weather to shape Earth. Over long periods of time, wind wore away some of the surrounding rocks, leaving behind these mini-mountains. Wind, water, and glacial ice also cause erosion, meaning they can break off tiny bits of rock and carry them away.

Hurricanes These storms form over warm ocean waters and have winds of at least 74 miles per hour (119 km/h). With howling winds, pelting rains, and powerful tides, they can really pack a punch. When hurricanes reach land, they erode beaches and destroy sand dunes. **Hurricane Katrina**, which affected Louisiana, Mississippi, Alabama, and Florida in 2005, caused more than 1,800 deaths and $160 billion in damage. It's hard to imagine a positive effect, but these destructive storms can also unearth new food supplies for scavenger animals, disperse plant seeds, and move sand to shore up barrier islands.

PINNACLES

HURRICANE KATRINA

Earthquakes Faults are places where two tectonic plates meet. As the plates scrape against each other, the resulting friction and heat can create earthquakes. A quake can produce tsunamis (giant waves) at sea and landslides on land, and sometimes they make soil lose its strength and act more like a liquid, causing buildings to collapse. But there are natural benefits to these destructive events. They release pressure under the surface, and when they shake up soil, it can spread its nutrients out more widely.

EARTHQUAKES

VOLCANOES

WHAT DOES A VOLCANO SAY ON VALENTINE'S DAY? I LAVA YOU!

Volcanoes When a volcano erupts, its lava can burn up or carry away everything in its path, wiping out entire forests and even towns. An enormous eruption can have a chilling effect, too. The **clouds of ash** that rise into the air can block the sun's radiation, cooling the average temperature by several degrees and changing the weather around Earth. On the plus side, as volcanic materials break down, they form good soil for growing food.

EWW!
THE BIG FLUSH

When Hurricane Sandy hit New York City in 2012, it unleashed more than 10 billion gallons (3.8 billion l) of sewage into waterways, onto streets, and inside homes in the area. One report estimated that if the sewage was spread out over Manhattan's Central Park, the pile would be 41 feet (12.5 m) high!

THAT'S ACTIVE!

SLIPPERY SLOPE

An AVALANCHE occurs when masses of fresh snow slide over an icy layer and then fall down a mountainside. Warmer temperatures, snowmelt, earthquakes, and even skiing can cause enough vibrations to trigger an avalanche that can race down a mountain at up to 200 miles per hour (320 km/h).

BIG WAVES

Surfers crave waves, and the coastline of NAZARÉ, Portugal, is where experienced extreme surfers go. A deep underwater canyon, ocean swells, and the crashing together of large waves as they approach the coast work together to form monster waves here that are 100 feet (30 m) high. So far, the big wave surfing record is an 86-foot (26.21-m) wave.

LIVELY LAVA

When Krakatoa, on Rakata Island in Indonesia, erupted in 1883, it was its first eruption in about 200 years. The sound could be heard in Australia, more than 2,000 miles (3,540 km) away! The entire island was destroyed by the explosion. But a new volcanic island—called **ANAK KRAKATAU** (child of Krakatoa)—rose in its place.

BLUSTERY BLIZZARDS

For a **BLIZZARD** to form, there needs to be a perfect storm of conditions: fresh or lightweight snow falling with sustained winds blowing at least 35 miles per hour (56 km/h) and low visibility—when you can't see more than 1,300 feet (400 m) in front of you. Some of the largest blizzards in the United States occur on the East Coast. In the winter months, cold arctic winds meet up with warm air over the Atlantic Ocean, generating blustery blizzards called nor'easters.

TSUNAMI TROUBLES

TSUNAMIS are a result of underwater earthquakes caused by the movement of tectonic plates. They create a sudden swell or surge of water that races through the ocean at up to 500 miles per hour (805 km/h). Sometimes a tsunami's trough—or low point—of a wave hits land first, sucking water away from the shore. Then water rushes in with a vengeance, wrecking everything in its path.

SIZZLING BRIGHT

A bolt of **LIGHTNING** strikes about 100 times every second on our planet. That means there are 6,000 strikes in one minute! Lightning is five times hotter than the surface of the sun, and there's enough electricity in a single lightning bolt to power a house for one month.

> WHAT DID THE CLOUD SAY ABOUT LIGHTNING? IT'S ILLUMINATING!

119

PICK A STAR AND MAKE A WISH!

ONE OF A KIND | There are billions of stars in our galaxy, but the sun is the only star in our solar system. It's not the largest of all stars, but it provides Earth with all the light, heat, and energy we need.

Chapter 7

SPACE

If you had a pen pal in outer space, they'd need more than your street address to send you a birthday card. They'd need something like this:

Earth ★ Solar System ★ Oort Cloud
Local Fluff ★ Local Bubble ★
Orion Arm ★ Milky Way Galaxy
Local Group ★ Virgo Supercluster
Laniakea Supercluster ★ Universe

This is your cosmic address—one that you share with everyone else on the planet. Get ready to explore your cosmic community.

OUR NEIGHBORS IN SPACE

Earth is one of eight planets in our solar system. From closest to farthest from the sun, they are Mercury, Venus, Earth, Mars, Jupiter, Saturn, Uranus, and Neptune. There are also dwarf planets, many moons, and space rocks such as asteroids, comets, and meteoroids.

Inner Planets The four planets closest to the sun are Mercury, Venus, Earth, and Mars. Called terrestrial planets, these inner planets have hard, rocky surfaces and are relatively small.

Outer Planets Jupiter, Saturn, Uranus, and Neptune are made mostly of gases. The largest of the outer planets are Jupiter and Saturn, known as gas giants. The two farthest from the sun are Uranus and Neptune, and these ice giants are super cold—less than -300°F (-184°C)!

Pluto and Pals Dwarf planets are smaller than our eight planets, but they share some characteristics: they orbit (circle around) the sun, and they have enough gravity to form a rounded shape. Unlike true planets, they don't have enough gravity to keep other objects out of their orbit path. There are five known dwarf planets: Pluto, Eris, Ceres, Makemake, and Haumea. Pluto was considered a regular planet until 2006, when it was reclassified.

The Moon The moon is our only natural satellite (such as a moon or planet that orbits a planet or star). The moon lights up our night sky, but it doesn't make its own light— that's sunlight bouncing off the moon's rocky surface. All the planets in our solar system have moons, except Mercury and Venus. Jupiter has 80 moons and Saturn has 83!

Asteroids These bits of rock are leftovers from the creation of the solar system many billions of years ago. Most orbit the sun in a belt located between Mars and Jupiter. When an asteroid encounters Earth's atmosphere, it usually burns up as it enters. Any pieces that make it through the atmosphere and land on Earth are called meteorites.

Comets These frozen balls of gases and rock whiz through space. When they get close to the sun and start to warm up, the comets form bright tails that we can see from Earth. Some comets pass by more than once. The most famous of these is Halley's Comet, which passes by about every 76 years. Mark your calendar: it's due for its next flyby in 2061 or 2062.

SUPER SPINNER

You can't feel it, but Earth is spinning at hundreds of miles per hour. The planet makes a full rotation on its axis (an imaginary straight line from the North Pole to the South Pole) every 24 hours.

PLUTO AND PALS

ASTEROID

COMET

AN EASY WAY TO REMEMBER THE PLANET ORDER IS: MY VERY EAGER MOTHER JUST SERVED US NACHOS!

NEPTUNE

URANUS

SATURN

JUPITER

MARS

THE SUN

EARTH

VENUS

MERCURY

MISSION TO MARS

Mars has fascinated humans for thousands of years. Is there life on the planet? Could we live there? Perhaps! It is more like Earth than any other planet, has a day about as long as ours, and has water in the form of ice below the planet's surface. But there are still some challenges: it can get cold—down to -220° F (-140° C) in some places—and it has very little oxygen.

The National Space and Aeronautics Agency (NASA) hopes to send the first crewed mission to Mars in the 2030s. It won't be easy! The trip will take about six months *each way*. And before the astronauts leave Earth, they must go through years of testing and training. Tons of equipment for their mission needs to be delivered to Mars, too. To make that possible, NASA plans first to build a permanent base on the moon that will serve as an eventual stopover point for trips to Mars. This base will also help scientists learn the best ways to prepare for future human exploration of deep space.

Countdown to the Moon and Beyond

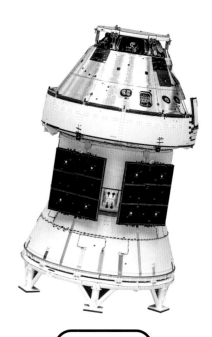

NASA's Space Launch System (SLS) is the world's most powerful rocket, designed to send astronauts, cargo, and the **Orion** spacecraft to the moon in a single trip. According to NASA, *Orion* has three components: a crew module, where astronauts will live, work, and control the spacecraft; a service module, which provides power, propulsion (pushing the craft forward), and water and air for the crew; and a launch abort system for emergencies during the launch or ascent.

In November 2022, the SLS megarocket launched *Orion* on its first test flight, a 25-day trip around the moon and back to Earth. There were no humans aboard, but it carried three models fitted with sensors to test how a human body would react to the journey to Mars. *Orion* will eventually carry astronauts to Mars.

ORION

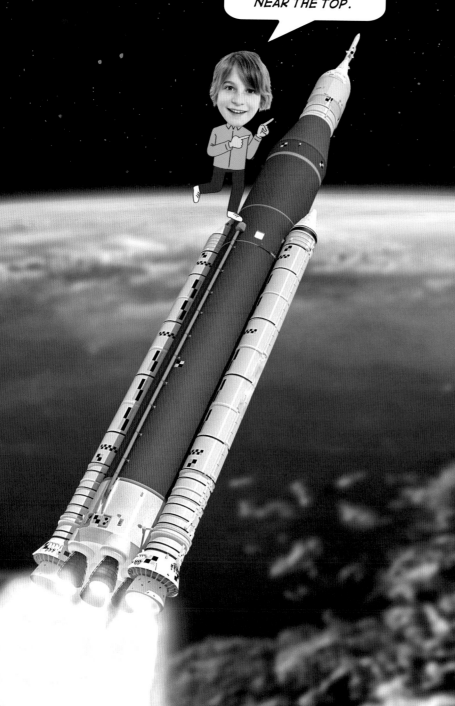

QUIZ
PLANET PARTICULARS

Test your knowledge of your galactic neighborhood with these true-or-false statements.

1. **ALL PLANETS IN OUR SOLAR SYSTEM HAVE MOONS.**

2. **PLUTO IS SMALLER THAN THE UNITED STATES.**

3. **JUPITER CLEANS UP SPACE OBJECTS IN ITS NEIGHBORHOOD.**

4. **SPACE IS NOISY.**

5. **MERCURY, THE CLOSEST PLANET TO THE SUN, IS TOO HOT FOR ICE.**

Answers are on page 157.

GREAT BALL OF FIRE

The sun is the superstar at the center of our solar system. This fiery ball of hot, glowing gas is made mostly of hydrogen and helium and contains plasma (a superheated state of matter). It's the biggest object in the solar system: it has 333,000 times as much mass as Earth. It sits 93 million miles (150 million km) away from our planet, but it takes just 8 minutes 20 seconds for sunlight to reach us. Like Earth, the sun has several active layers below its surface.

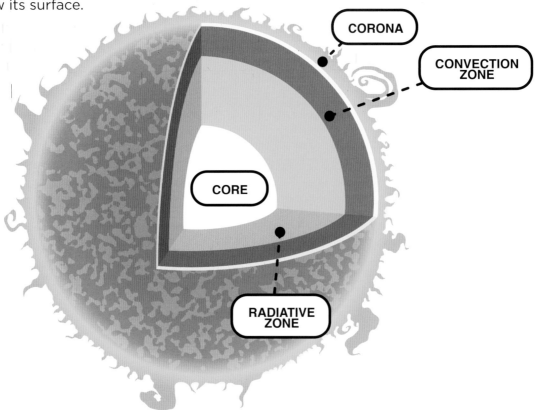

Core At this hot spot, the sun is 27 million°F (15 million°C). This is where the sun's energy is created and stored.

Radiative Zone The sun's energy moves outward through the radiative zone over thousands of years, losing about 85% of its heat.

Convection Zone Bubbling plasma moves the sun's energy farther away from its core. This process, called convection, is the upward movement of hot gas or liquid and the downward movement of cooler gas or liquid, like water boiling in a pot.

Corona The outermost layer is big, but the sun's bright light makes it impossible to see with the naked eye. The squiggle shapes that extend from the corona are called solar streamers—they extend millions of miles into space.

Earth's BFF

The sun's energy lights up our planet and warms our atmosphere and bodies of water, which makes our planet habitable. No doubt about it, without the sun our planet would be dark and icy cold. The sun also creates winds and ocean currents, influences seasons and climates, and drives the water cycle (how water keeps changing from liquid to gas to solid), too. Its energy can be used for cooking, and when converted to electricity it can power our homes, schools, and factories.

DIY

CATCH SOME RAYS

Let the sunshine in and capture its light with a suncatcher! To make one, you'll need a clear plastic lid (from a food container); craft glue; and shiny sequins, beads, or pieces of colored glass.

Cover one side of the lid with the glue, add your shiny materials, and set the suncatcher aside to dry. When it's completely dry, set it by a sunny window and see how it catches the sun's light.

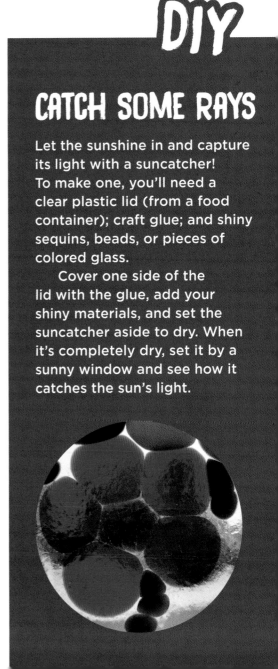

Sun Worship

No one knows for sure why a group of stone pillars weighing an average of 25 tons (23 mt) were erected in a circle on the Salisbury Plain in England some 5,000 years ago. But many believe it had some sort of astronomical purpose. On the summer solstice each year, the rising sun shines through Stonehenge's center. Thousands gather at this site to celebrate the sun on the longest day of the year.

A STELLAR LIFE

A star is born in a nebula—a huge, spinning cloud of gas and dust. This earliest form is called a protostar. It then follows one of two paths.

1. Low-mass (smaller) stars burn slowly and live long lives—in the billions of years. Our sun is a low-mass star, and it is 4.6 billion years old. As it grows, a low-mass star develops a core and begins emitting energy (light and heat). After billions of years, it begins to lose energy and sheds its outer material (which becomes a planetary nebula). What remains is a tightly packed core known as a white dwarf, which is about the size of Earth.

2. High-mass stars burn fast and live short lives—in the millions of years. Betelgeuse, in the constellation Orion, is a high-mass star. These stars are ten times as massive as our sun. Over millions of years, these supergiants burn increasingly hotter and brighter until, eventually, the core collapses in a giant explosion called a supernova. High-mass stars leave behind either a neutron star (its core) or a black hole.

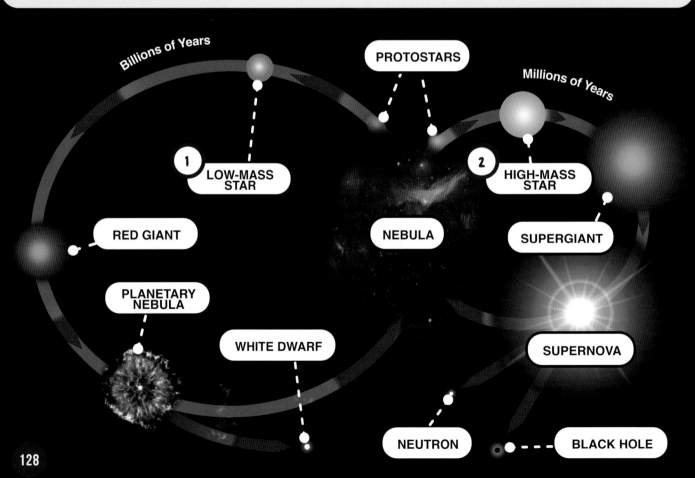

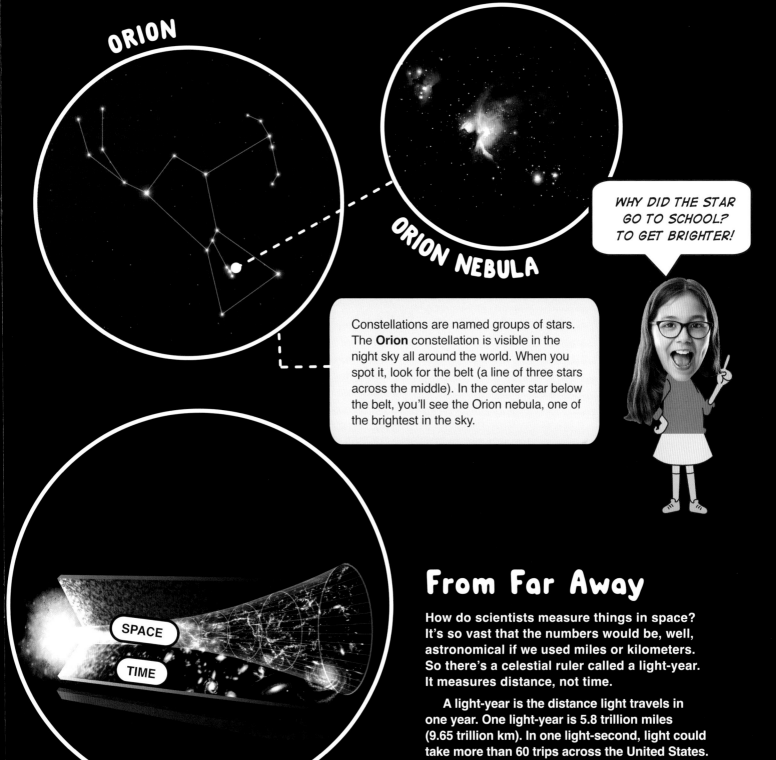

ORION

ORION NEBULA

WHY DID THE STAR GO TO SCHOOL? TO GET BRIGHTER!

Constellations are named groups of stars. The **Orion** constellation is visible in the night sky all around the world. When you spot it, look for the belt (a line of three stars across the middle). In the center star below the belt, you'll see the Orion nebula, one of the brightest in the sky.

SPACE

TIME

From Far Away

How do scientists measure things in space? It's so vast that the numbers would be, well, astronomical if we used miles or kilometers. So there's a celestial ruler called a light-year. It measures distance, not time.

A light-year is the distance light travels in one year. One light-year is 5.8 trillion miles (9.65 trillion km). In one light-second, light could take more than 60 trips across the United States.

GALACTIC GRANDEUR

A galaxy contains billions of stars and their solar systems, dust, and gases. It's held together by gravity, which pulls everything in it toward its center. There are more than 50 galaxies of different shapes and sizes in our Local Group (a group of galaxies that includes the Milky Way), and scientists estimate there could be 200 billion galaxies—and possibly many more—in the vast universe!

BARRED SPIRAL

YOU ARE HERE

SPIRAL

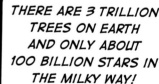

Spiral Our nearest large galactic neighbor is the **Andromeda galaxy**. It's 2.5 million light-years away—right next door in space terms. It has a bulging center and clusters of baby stars (which are blue) and star nurseries.

Barred Spiral Our galaxy, the **Milky Way**, has a long bar-shaped center with arms radiating out from the ends. Hundreds of billions of stars swirl in a spiral, with most clustered in the yellowish center. Scientists have discovered a vast number of stellar nurseries—places where new stars are born—within the Milky Way.

THERE ARE 3 TRILLION TREES ON EARTH AND ONLY ABOUT 100 BILLION STARS IN THE MILKY WAY!

IRREGULAR

Irregular These starry galaxies don't appear organized or structured. Scientists believe some may form when galaxies collide. The **Large Magellanic Cloud**, an irregular galaxy, contains vast clouds of gas and a starburst called the Tarantula nebula, which is the largest star-forming region in our Local Group.

WOW!

BUBBLE BUBBLE

Something happened at the center of our galaxy several million years ago that created two giant bubbles of gas. They seem to emerge from the center of the Milky Way and may be related to the black hole at the center of our galaxy. Called the Fermi Bubbles, these colorful, giant blobs of gas are moving at 2 million miles per hour (3.2 million km/h)!

ELLIPTICAL

Elliptical These oval galaxies are dim and less dense than spirals because there is less dust and gas, and they form few or no new stars. For these reasons, scientists think they are older than spirals. The elliptical galaxy **Cygnus-A** clearly shows the red color that older stars emit.

BLACK HOLES

Black Holes The Milky Way has a **black hole** at its center—in fact, scientists think most galaxies have one. But it isn't an empty hole. Huge amounts of matter are jammed into a tiny space, and its gravity is so strong that it continually pulls interstellar matter like gases and dust toward it and nothing can get out. Most often, a black hole is created when a giant star dies out in brilliant flash of light called a supernova.

THE SPACE SUPERHIGHWAY

Human beings have been stargazers for thousands of years. Scientists think some early cave paintings were actually depictions of constellations. From telescopes to rovers (robotic vehicles for exploring moon or planet surfaces), we have amazing tools of discovery to find out what's up above.

Juno This NASA spacecraft reached Jupiter and began its orbit around the planet in 2016, but it launched from Earth five years earlier, in 2011. **Juno's** mission is to help us learn about Jupiter's history and conditions, including the atmosphere, magnetic field, and massive storms like the Great Red Spot.

Hubble Telescope This eye in the sky has been orbiting about 340 miles (547 km) above Earth's surface for more than 30 years. It has transmitted more than a million incredibly detailed images of its discoveries, including nebulae, galaxies, **star clusters**, and planets.

FAST Five-Hundred-Meter Aperture Spherical Telescope is massive—it scans the skies with a dish that is 1,640 feet (500 m) wide. That's as long as 30 soccer fields. Located in China, it detects cosmic energy using radio waves. Some of the signals it receives are from pulsars, which are rapidly spinning neutron stars.

Perseverance Mars Rover The rover's main mission is to look for signs of ancient life on Mars. **Perseverance** also carried a small helicopter named **Ingenuity**. This whirlybird took a flight in 2021. It made history as the first powered, controlled flight of an aircraft on another planet in our solar system.

ISS The International Space Station orbits about 240 miles (386 km) above Earth's surface. It takes 90 minutes to orbit our planet, completing 16 orbits a day. Astronauts conduct experiments on board, and their **space walks** outside the ISS let them test new equipment and make repairs to the spacecraft.

EWW!

TO BOLDLY GO

We've got to know: how do astronauts go to the bathroom in space? The ISS space toilets use suction, so nothing ends up, um, floating in space. Another cool feature: there's a built-in pee treatment system on board that converts urine to water that's safe for the astronauts to drink and use. The poop is packed into canisters, loaded onto a cargo ship that brought supplies, and sent back to Earth, where it burns up when it reenters our atmosphere.

THE WORLDWIDE WEBB

The James Webb Space Telescope transmitted its first images of the universe to Earth in July 2022. Its pictures revealed parts of the universe no one had seen before.

Building the world's largest and most powerful space telescope was no easy feat. Scientists and engineers from more than a dozen countries worked for 14 years to assemble it. Webb is a unique telescope because it doesn't just see objects in space. It also can look back in time. But how? Some galaxies are so far from Earth that the light they create takes billions of years to travel through space. We see them as they were when the light first began to travel. Webb captures what those galaxies looked like billions of years ago. Plus, it has special sensors that detect infrared light, a kind of light that isn't visible to the human eye.

Close-Up Cuties For the first time, we can see mountainlike regions and glittery individual stars within the Carina nebula nursery, shining a new light on how stars are born. This nebula has given birth to some stars that are at least 50 times more massive than Earth's sun.

Jumping Gymnastics Webb took a peek inside the Cartwheel galaxy to reveal secrets previously hidden. Its wheel shape formed during a high-speed collision with two other galaxies, it has a black hole at its center, and its outer ring is a hub of star formation.

Galactic Get-Together Another first, this image of Stephan's Quintet gives a close-up look at what happens when multiple galaxies meet and interact. One of the galaxies is smashing through the group, and there's evidence of gas disturbances in the galaxies that may show how galaxies age and change over time.

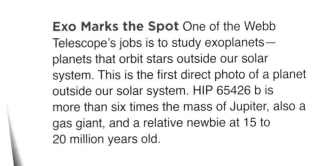

PLANET

Exo Marks the Spot One of the Webb Telescope's jobs is to study exoplanets—planets that orbit stars outside our solar system. This is the first direct photo of a planet outside our solar system. HIP 65426 b is more than six times the mass of Jupiter, also a gas giant, and a relative newbie at 15 to 20 million years old.

In the Spotlight The largest and brightest star-forming area of our very own Local Group is the Tarantula nebula. Never-before-seen young blue stars twinkle in its center, surrounded by wispy curls that resemble woven spider-silk. The Tarantula nebula is a hotbed of activity, producing new stars at a faster rate than the Milky Way.

THAT'S FaR oUt!

THE EVER-EXPANDING DAY

A day lasts 24 hours, right? Well, it hasn't always been that way. The **LENGTH OF THE DAY** depends on how quickly Earth completes one rotation on its axis, and the moon sets the pace. The moon is slowly moving away from us—about 1 inch (2.5 cm) every year. The farther away the moon is, the slower Earth rotates, making a day longer. More than 1 billion years ago, when the moon was closer, a day lasted just 18 hours. Talk about not having enough time in the day!

SPOT SPINNER

What's that **GREAT RED SPOT** on Jupiter? It's actually a supersize storm that has been spinning over the planet for hundreds of years. It's 10,000 miles (16,000 km) across, about the width of Earth. But it's been shrinking for at least 100 years—it used to be as big as three Earths—and no one knows why. It "eats" other storms that form over Jupiter and uses their energy to keep spinning. In some places, the wind reaches 400 miles per hour (644 km/h)—about 25% stronger than the most powerful tornadoes on Earth.

SPINNING THROUGH SPACE

Objects in the universe can spin, or rotate, at incredible speeds. Earth orbits the sun at about 67,000 miles per hour (107,000 km/h)—at that speed we could get from here to the moon in just under four hours!
A spiral galaxy, like our **MILKY WAY**, spins in some places at a rapid 130 miles per second (210 km/sec). At that speed, the same moon trip would take about 30 minutes!

BLOCK THAT LIGHT

When Earth, moon, and sun line up in the sky, they cause a **TOTAL SOLAR ECLIPSE**. It's like flipping off the light switch on Earth. But why? The moon is a lot smaller than the sun, but because the moon is much closer to Earth, they appear to us to be about the same size. When these three objects are in just the right position, the moon blocks the sun's light for about eight minutes. This can cause confusion. Some spiders even start taking apart their webs, as they usually do at the end of the day.

SENSATIONAL CENTAURI

After our star, the sun, the closest star to Earth is **PROXIMA CENTAURI**. It's in Alpha Centauri, the closest solar system to ours. Orbiting Proxima Centauri is the closest exoplanet, Proxima Centauri b. Like Earth, it's a rocky planet, about the same size, and a similar distance to its star. Hmm . . . could it possibly support life? It would take more than 6,000 years to get there, so don't plan on a visit just yet.

FLARES UP THERE

The sun's surface is incredibly active. Continual explosions release a kind of energy called electromagnetic radiation, causing intense flashes of light called **SOLAR FLARES**. When some of this energy reaches Earth as solar storms, they can disrupt technology such as radar and satellites.

137

EACH PYRAMID BLOCK WEIGHS AS MUCH AS ME. THAT'S HEAVY!

THAT'S IMPRESSIVE | One of the most amazing engineering projects was completed more than 4,500 years ago. The Great Pyramid of Giza in Egypt was constructed from more than 2 million blocks of stone, each weighing about 5,000 pounds (2,268 kg). It took 20 years and more than 20,000 workers to complete it using only simple machines.

Chapter 8

ENGINEERING & TECHNOLOGY

Engineering uses science, math, and technology to solve problems and figure out new ways of doing things. Engineers design and create the buildings we live and work in, thrilling amusement park rides that are also safe, sports equipment that keeps us safe while active, medical innovations like artificial body parts that assist people who need them, robotic spacecraft that can explore the distant universe, and solar energy systems to harness the sun's energy and convert it to electricity. Here's a look at some of the vast number of ways engineering and technology shape our lives.

MACHINES AT WORK

Thousands of years ago, engineers invented six simple machines that make work easier by creating or changing motion and increasing force: inclined plane, lever, pulley, screw, wedge, and the wheel and axle. Two or more simple machines can work together in what engineers call a compound machine. Today, an automobile is made from thousands of individual pieces, making it a complicated compound machine. But it couldn't work without these six simple machines.

Inclined Plane It requires less work to push an object up or down a slope than to lift and carry it across a flat surface. On a car, the slope of the windshield is designed to deflect rain and to reduce drag (a force that slows down motion).

Lever A rigid beam on a pivot point called a fulcrum helps lift more weight with less force. When a driver flips on a turn signal, that's a lever at work. So are the windshield wipers.

Pulley A combination of one or more wheels with a rope or cable makes it easier to raise, lower, and pull objects. You use this simple machine when you put on a seatbelt. A fan belt in the engine helps to power the car, makes the steering mechanisms work, and keeps the engine—and you—cool.

Screw When you turn a screw so it goes into a solid object, the threads (ridges) convert the rotational force of you turning it into linear force. Screws hold car parts together. Without screws, the wheels of a car would fall off. And headlight and taillight bulbs screw into sockets.

Wedge A wedge is shaped like a triangle, and combines two inclined planes that taper to a narrow edge or point. The lock on a seatbelt is a wedge, as is the ignition key, which gets the car started.

Wheel and Axle This machine involves a rod (called an axle) and one or more wheels that revolve around it. In a car, an axle connects each pair of wheels. A steering wheel is also connected to an axle and turns the car's wheels. Trucks, tractors, and trailers can have more wheels and axles.

WOW!

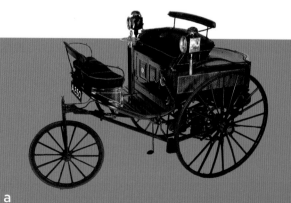

A TRUE ORIGINAL

In 1886, a German engineer named Karl Benz patented the first gasoline-powered car. It had three wheels—one up front for steering and two in back for support. There were no gas stations, so drivers bought gasoline at a drugstore or a hardware or grocery store. In its first five years of production, Benz's company produced 25 cars. Today, about 66 million new cars are sold worldwide in a year. That's more than 50,000 per day!

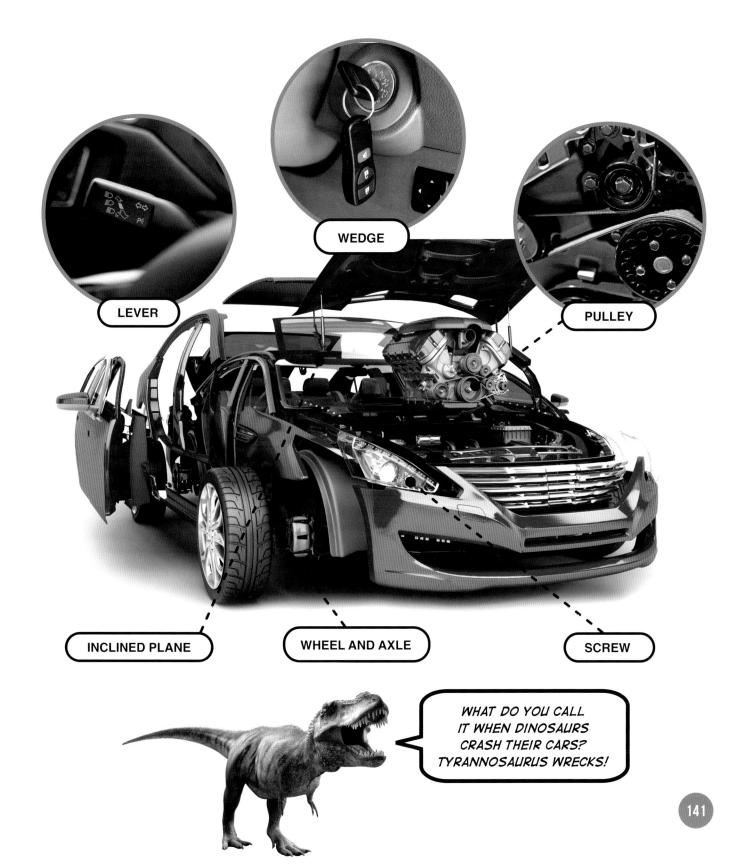

WEDGE

LEVER

PULLEY

INCLINED PLANE

WHEEL AND AXLE

SCREW

WHAT DO YOU CALL IT WHEN DINOSAURS CRASH THEIR CARS? TYRANNOSAURUS WRECKS!

FROM DRIVEWAY TO HIGHWAY

A car is made up several different systems that help it go, stop, steer, and keep passengers safe.

Brakes Stop! Brakes rely on friction—a pad or disc presses against a wheel to slow it down. An anti-locking brake system (ABS) automatically pumps (engages and releases) the brakes during a sudden stop, to prevent skidding and give the driver greater control.

Chassis and Body The chassis is the frame that holds all the car's systems together. The body sits on the chassis and protects everything inside the car.

Electronics Cars today rely on computers to control many of their functions. One of their jobs is to make adjustments in the engine to reduce pollution; another is to diagnose why a car isn't running right and what needs to be fixed.

Exhaust Cars on the move give off exhaust, a by-product of a running engine that can include a mixture of chemicals, such as nitrogen, oxygen, and water. It passes through the exhaust system and tailpipe on its way out of the car.

Suspension and Steering The steering controls the direction of a car and the suspension provides support and absorbs shock from the tires and roadway. They keep the car stable and ensure a smooth ride.

Transmission This system takes the power created in the engine and delivers it to the wheels so they move.

SNORKEL

Off-Road Outfit

Vehicles designed to drive in rough conditions—wading through shallow rivers and streams and across sand— need a way to bring air to the engine. A snorkel reaches up along the side of the car to "breathe" in dry air. These vehicles also have bigger tires that are designed to absorb the bumps and dips, with treads and edges designed to grip uneven terrain and handle muddy or sandy conditions.

Engine Ignition

Internal combustion engines are what make most cars go. With the turn of a key or push of a start button, an ignition switch generates voltage in a battery that creates a spark to ignite a mixture of air and gasoline. This creates a gas that makes a piston move, and that energy is transferred to the wheels. Electric cars use batteries and motors instead of internal combustion engines, and hybrids have both gasoline-powered engines and electric motors.

INTAKE

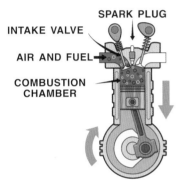

- Air and fuel mixture is drawn in
- Intake valve open

COMPRESSION

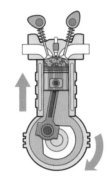

- Air and fuel mixture is compressed
- Intake and exhaust valve closed

POWER

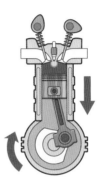

- Spark plug firing
- Explosion forces piston down
- Intake and exhaust valve closed

EXHAUST

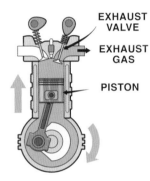

- Piston pushes out burned gases
- Exhaust valve open

QUIZ
COUPE SCOOP

Can you tell fact from fiction in this cool car true-or-false quiz?

1. FRENCH FRIES CAN PROVIDE FUEL FOR CARS.

2. CARS CAN'T RUN FOR MORE THAN 500,000 MILES (804,672 KM).

3. THE FASTEST CAR EVER TRAVELED JUST UNDER 500 MILES PER HOUR (805 KM/H).

4. THE FIRST CARS INVENTED DIDN'T HAVE BRAKE LIGHTS.

For answers, see page 157.

CONSTRUCTION ZONE

When it comes to designing, building, and maintaining dams, tunnels, airports, water pipelines, and roadways, civil engineers take the lead. They make sure these public works are built safely, meet environmental laws, and will function well for the people who use them.

SKY HIGH

China's **Shanghai Tower** climbs up 2,073 feet (632 m). Engineers had to consider the area's naturally occurring storms and its location in an earthquake zone. The building is anchored in place by a deep concrete foundation and nearly 1,000 piles (support cylinders), to give it stability. Its twisted, rounded shape helps it withstand strong winds. It also has some climate-friendly features: two layers of glass for insulation, wind turbines on the roof to generate electricity, and a system to collect and recycle wastewater and rain.

Considered the greatest public works project in history, the **U.S. interstate highway system** began in 1956, when Congress passed a law to create a highway system that would make it possible for people and goods to travel quickly and safely from state to state. The interstate extends over more than 46,000 miles (74,000 km). The longest highway in the system is I-90, which traverses 13 states on its 3,085-mile (4,965 km) journey from Seattle to Boston. Including the interstate and other roadways, the United States has the largest network of roads in the world.

COAST TO COAST

UNFINISHED BUSINESS

Begun in 1882, **La Sagrada Familia** in Barcelona is the oldest and longest ongoing construction project. It's scheduled to be completed in 2026, and a recent addition is the placement of an illuminated star atop one of its towers.

This church is a masterpiece of architecture art and design, engineering, and math. To determine how much support certain parts of the building would need, its designer, a young architect named Antoni Gaudí, constructed a three-dimensional model, with elements built to scale to represent actual weight-bearing capabilities. Today, architects use computers to solve these problems.

DAMMED UP

UP AND OVER

The Millau Bridge in France is the tallest bridge in the world. It's 1,125 feet (343 m) high, making it taller than the Eiffel Tower. It's also the longest cable-stayed bridge, at 8,071 feet (2,460 m). It has cables and pylons (towers) that hold up the steel deck (roadway), which rests on seven concrete pillars sunk deep into the ground. This engineering marvel turned a four-hour drive to get around a steep gorge into a trip of just a few minutes.

Beavers—nature's engineers—are experts at building **dams** in streams. The dammed water creates a small pond for their large structures that are made of logs, sticks, and plants. Inside, there's a large, dry room where the beavers live and raise babies. Underwater entrances keep them safe from predators. And thick layers of vegetation and the sun's warmth help keep the lodge the right temperature for its inhabitants.

SOLAR AND SUSTAINABLE

Engineers and other technologists put their brainpower to work inventing ways to solve problems. For example, figuring out systems to help organizations and people conserve energy, reuse materials, and clean up the planet is one way they help make our lives, and futures, better.

Solar Sailing Just as wind pushes against the sails of a boat to move it through water, sunlight pushed the sails of an experimental craft through space. **LightSail2**, launched in 2019, was about the size of a loaf of bread. It had 433-square-foot (23-sq-m) sails—about the size of a boxing ring— and was powered by tiny particles of light energy called photons. The force of the photons bouncing off the sail's shiny material pushed the craft through space. Orbiting Earth for more than three years, this was the first successful experiment with solar sailing.

Print It! Designers and engineers use **3D printers** to create models, which can then also be used to make actual homes. This two-story home was constructed using a very large printer that pumped out concrete in layers. The 3D printer uses computers and specialized software for design and construction. These homes are quicker and less expensive to build than homes that are built with traditional methods and materials, which saves energy and reduces the number of trees harvested for lumber.

River Revival Trash travels down rivers on its way to the ocean. Removing it before it reaches the ocean is the goal of solar-powered floating garbage collectors. Anchored in place in the Baltimore Harbor in Maryland, **Mr. Trash Wheel** runs on water and solar power. It has a 14-foot (4.3-m) waterwheel powered by currents, with backup solar power when waters are calm. The wheel moves rotating forks through the water to collect garbage, placing it on a conveyer belt that moves it to a storage area. The debris is later recycled. Mr. Trash Wheel has collected more than 2,000 tons (1,814 mt) of trash since 2014.

Air Purifier Smog—air in which fog has absorbed smoke, exhaust fumes from cars, and other pollutants—isn't healthy for humans, animals, or plants. How can we make the air we breathe cleaner? Meet the **smog vacuum cleaner**. This 23-foot (7-m) tower sucks in dirty air at the top and filters it, releasing clean air through vents on its sides.

Tire-d at Home Some special ships dot the landscape of northern New Mexico, but you can't sail in them. They're actually houses known as **earthships**. They're designed so that the people who live in them use as little energy and water as possible, and recycled goods are a big part of the building material. Used tires stuffed with dirt are the "bricks" used for the main walls. Some earthship builders also include repurposed metal and wood in their homes.

HYDRAULICS AND PNEUMATICS

These may sound very different, but they're related technologies. They put energy to work by combining the force of motion with a liquid or gas. Machines that rely on them may also be connected to an electrical system, but hydraulics and pneumatics make specific jobs easier to do in a controlled way.

Hydraulics

Energy can travel through fluids under pressure and can multiply the force of that pressure, too. Using hydraulics, a smaller amount of force in one place creates a larger, more powerful force somewhere else, making hydraulic systems ideal for large jobs and heavy lifting. Excavators, robotic systems in factories, and car and airplane steering systems rely on hydraulics. Most hydraulic systems use oil rather than water because it doesn't freeze, reduces friction to keep moving parts moving, and doesn't cause rust.

Pneumatics

Similar to hydraulics, this technology uses a gas—air—to transmit power from one part of a machine to another. Pneumatics is used for quick, repetitive tasks. When you push down on a bicycle pump, the air flows out. When you repeat the pumping motion, you send energy through the air under high pressure. The air then flows into the hose and through the nozzle into the tire to inflate it.

EXCAVATOR

BOOM

BUCKET

Big Digs A system of levers in the driver's cab moves fluid through cylinders, where it is converted to mechanical energy to move the boom and bucket.

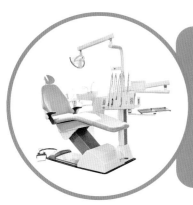

CHAIR LIFT The height of a dentist's chair needs to be easy for you to sit on, but it also needs to be higher for a dentist to do their work while standing. A foot pump or pedal gets a hydraulic system moving to lift the chair—and you—up. The drill uses pneumatics to turn a small turbine in the drill's head to spin a burr that drills into or shapes teeth. It runs on air power, which is cleaner for work done inside the mouth!

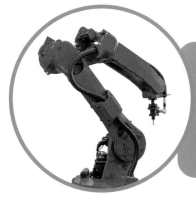

SET AND REPEAT Robotic arms are programmed by computers to make quick work of the repeated tasks in factories. They can be used to assemble cars, paint machinery, and load products onto conveyor belts. They have joints, like human arms, for a wide range of movement. Many industrial robots operate using hydraulics or pneumatics.

MAKING MONEY The coins in your pocket were stamped out of large sheets of metal known as blanks. Then hydraulic presses stamped the designs to both sides at the same time, using 39 to 110 tons (35 to 100 mt) of pressure. One press can produce 750 coins per minute.

A LARGE EXCAVATOR CAN WEIGH MORE THAN 40 TONS (36 MT)—AS MUCH AS NINE ELEPHANTS!

AMAZING DISCOVERIES

Engineering and technology can help us add new buildings, machines, and systems to our lives. They can also help us discover things that have long been hidden—such as ancient cities buried underground—or are naturally hard to spot, like nocturnal animals or organs inside the human body.

SURFACE VIEW

WITH LiDAR

LiDAR This remote sensing technology (LiDAR stands for light detection and radar) uses pulsing lasers. When they are aimed at an area, the light reflects back and the distance the light travels forms a 3D image. This technology is used on autonomous (driverless) cars as the "eyes" to detect objects in the vicinity. Amazingly, LiDAR can also be used to reveal things we can't see at all, like this 3,000-year-old Mayan structure. Without LiDAR, the only way to discover places like this would be by cutting down plants and trees and digging up the land—if we even knew where to start.

HIDDEN CAMERA

LEOPARD AT NIGHT

Camera Trap Learning about animals in the wild is easier with the help of cameras placed in their habitat. A digital camera outfitted with an infrared trigger senses an animal's heat and starts taking pictures. Hidden cameras record shy or nocturnal animals, as well as those that live in remote areas, without disturbing their natural behaviors.

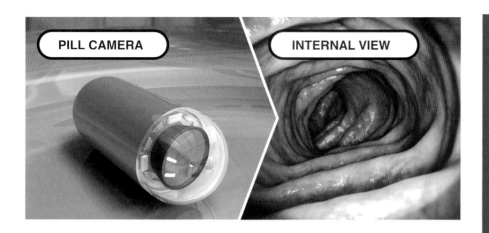

PILL CAMERA

INTERNAL VIEW

Pill Cam A tiny camera about the size of a pill gives doctors a way to see what's going on inside the human body. After you swallow it, its journey through your digestive system takes about eight hours. It can record up to 50,000 pictures and send them to sensors placed on your body. Most pill capsules use disposable cameras—they don't need to be recovered when they, um, leave your body.

SETTING MIC

BELUGA RECORDING

Hydrophone Do fish talk? Do currents rumble? How much noise do boats make below the surface? An underwater microphone recognizes pressure caused by sound waves and records these changes as electrical signals to measure these sounds. It floats in place, with a buoyant device at the surface and a weight like a chain at the bottom.

DIY

DESIGN TIME

To solve a problem like an engineer, follow these steps.

1. Analyze It
Break down a problem into simpler parts. Think about what each part is meant to do and if it does that successfully.

2. Be Creative
Ask questions that begin with "how" and "why." This will help you figure out what you can do to make changes and improvements.

3. Focus on Facts
Consider what you know is true and research what you don't yet know.

4. Don't Give Up
Some problems are harder to solve than others.

5. Figure It Out
Now, think about a task that seems hard, such as cleaning your room or doing a science project. Grab a pen and paper and start working through these steps to come up with ideas for how to solve the problem.

EXTREME ENGINEERING

Big projects, new inventions, and challenging situations call for creative thinking and innovative solutions. Here are some examples of amazing engineering.

EARTHQUAKE ZONE

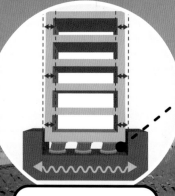

BASE ISOLATION

How to build for safety in an earthquake zone is a problem engineers addressed in several ways when designing **Apple's headquarters** in Silicon Valley, California. Earthquakes shake the ground, creating vibrations that can damage or topple buildings when they shake back and forth on their foundations. The large, circular building uses base isolators, which act like giant shock absorbers to reduce the impact of vibrations, and seismic expansion joints that also resist potential damaging effects.

FERRIS WHEEL

The first **Ferris wheel** was introduced at Chicago's 1893 Exposition. It was designed by George Ferris, a bridge and tunnel engineer. It was built from more than 100,000 parts, including 3,000 lights and a massive 89,320-pound (40,515-kg) axle at its center. Although Ferris built only one wheel, it was so impressive that his name became synonymous with this enormously popular amusement park ride.

SOLAR POWER STATION

Rising more than 800 feet (244 m) from the Negev Desert in Israel, the solar tower of Ashalim is so bright that it can be seen from space. It converts solar energy to electricity with the help of more than 50,000 mirrors. During the day, the mirrors reflect the sun's light to a water boiler at the top of the tower. The water boils and turns into steam, which travels to the tower's base, where it turns turbines to create electricity that can power more than 100,000 homes.

GLOBAL POSITIONING SYSTEM

For thousands of years, people used stars, compasses, and maps to navigate. But thanks to electrical engineering, people can now find their way around a new town, companies can track shipments on boats in the middle of the ocean, and farmers can guide tractors through fields remotely with the help of **GPS satellites** orbiting Earth. Ground stations use radar to send signals to the satellites, which then send signals to receivers in phones, cars, and other devices. With four or more satellite-receiver interactions, the receiver can determine locations with a high degree of accuracy.

INTERNATIONAL SPACE STATION

The largest construction project ever launched into space, the **ISS** took 13 years to build. It was built on Earth in modules that were launched into space, where they were joined together by robots and spacewalking astronauts. Home to seven astronauts at a time, this 35,000-cubic-foot (1,000-cu-m) laboratory has two bathrooms and living quarters about the size of a six-bedroom house.

153

THAT'S INVENTIVE!

SWISH-SWISH

In the winter of 1903, real estate developer Mary Anderson traveled by trolley car to New York City during a snowstorm. The driver had to open the windows and use his hands to wipe snow and ice from the windshield. Inspired, Anderson designed a device with a swinging arm and a rubber blade that worked with a lever inside the car. She received a patent (a statement from the government that her invention was unique and belonged to her) for the first working WINDSHIELD WIPER in 1903.

HELPING HAND

A BIONIC HAND or arm may sound like something out of a sci-fi movie, but with the help of robotic technology, prosthetics (artificial body parts) can help people who have lost a limb. Electric signals from the brain are sent to a computer in the mechanical limb, directing its movement. Sensors can send signals back to the brain, giving the person better control.

AQUATIC AVIATION

HYDROFLYING uses the propulsion (the force) of a pressurized stream of water to lift a board—and rider—up to 50 feet (15 m) in the air. Rather than having its own motor, the board relies on a personal watercraft like a Jet Ski that sucks up water and pumps it through a hose, generating enough force to send the board—and rider—airborne. The hose is attached to the board and has a device that allows the rider to lower the pressure for a safe landing. While many models exist today, the first—called a Flyboard—was invented in 2011 by Franky Zapata.

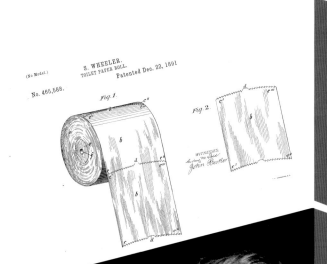

ON A ROLL

It's hard to imagine living without toilet paper. In 1871, Seth Wheeler invented the modern **TOILET PAPER ROLL** wrapped around a cardboard tube, and in 1891 he devised a way to make it perforated, so sheets could be pulled off in small sections. Wheeler received more than 100 patents for his invention. His Albany Perforated Wrapping Paper Co. was very successful, and he wound up being very rich.

TW-ICE AS NICE

An edible treat was invented by accident when 11-year-old Frank Epperson left a cup of fruit-flavored soda with a stirring stick outside overnight. It froze into an icicle-like sweet treat. But Epperson didn't recognize this as an invention for nearly two decades, when he finally applied for a patent and began making Eppsicles. He eventually changed the name to **POPSICLE**, and after two years sold his ice pop rights to another company. He celebrated his invention's 50th anniversary with his granddaughter.

STARDUST

How do you catch **COMET PARTICLES** in space? NASA's Stardust spacecraft used a special material called aerogel to catch bits of comet dust and bring them back to Earth. While it works like foam—fast-moving particles sink into the material when they hit it—it's actually a material unlike any other. Using high heat and pressure, the liquid in this silicon-based gel is transformed into gas. This process, called supercritical drying, created what is called the world's lightest solid.

QUIZ ANSWERS

ANIMALS
PAGE 29

1. False. Domesticated cats and small wild cats purr. Big wild cats, like lions and tigers, can't. But big cats can roar, while the smaller cats can't.
2. True. Scratching things is one way cats mark their territory, using scent glands in their paws. Domesticated cats also scratch to remove dead nail coverings, and to stretch their front legs and spine.
3. False. Lion cubs, cougars, cheetahs, and snow leopards meow too.
4. True and false. Cats both hiss and growl to say, "Back off!"

NATURE
PAGE 41

1. With an outer skin, soft flesh, and a pit, avocado is a fruit.
2. The seeds inside green beans make them a fruit.
3. Olives are a fruit—vegetables don't have pits.
4. Rhubarb is a vegetable, but add strawberries and it makes a great dessert pie.
5. Yup, spinach is a vegetable.
6. Watermelon is a vegetable. In fact, it's the state vegetable of Oklahoma.

HUMAN BODY
PAGE 61

1. False. Giraffes, humans, and nearly all mammals have seven bones in their neck.
2. False. You were born with about 300 bones. As you grow, some of the bones fuse (join together). For example, the humerus forms from separate bones that combine into a single, fully formed upper arm bone over about 10 years. By the time you're in your 20s, you'll be down to 206 bones.
3. True, but it's close. People have 27 bones in each hand and 26 bones in each foot.
4. False. The shortest bone is the stapes, in your inner ear. The longest is the femur, your thigh bone.

ENERGY
PAGE 93

1. False. They both travel at the same speed: 186,000 miles per second (299,792,458 m/s).
2. True. Your heart's electrical system sends signals to make it beat about 60 to 100 times each minute.
3. True. Electric eels use a short electric jolt to make their prey flop around, so it's easier to spot, then a second, stronger jolt that paralyzes the meal.
4. True. Several inventors worked together to create the popper, which soon became POPular. Also new to American homes in the first few years of the 20th century were the vacuum cleaner, air conditioner, and radio.

EARTH
PAGE 103

1. False. All terrestrial dinosaurs died off 66 million years ago, but the birds you see today are living descendants of dinosaurs.

2. True. Thousands of feathered dinosaurs have been discovered. Some scientists think all dinosaurs had feathers.

3. False. *Stegosaurus* lived more than 80 million years before *T. rex* evolved.

4. True. Water has been on Earth for billions of years, and it continually evaporates, condenses, and precipitates.

SPACE
PAGE 125

1. False. There are more than 150 moons in our solar system, and only Mercury and Venus are moon-free.

2. True. Pluto's diameter is about half the diameter of the United States (from coast to coast).

3. True. Its gravity field sucks in so many asteroids that it's nicknamed the vacuum cleaner of the solar system.

4. False. There's no air in space, so there's no way for sound to travel.

5. False. There's ice in shadowed craters on Mercury. Scientists think it may come from crashing icy comets.

ENGINEERING & TECHNOLOGY
PAGE 143

1. True . . . sort of. Oil used to cook the fries can be recycled and turned into a fuel called biodiesel.

2. False. The current Guinness World Record for vehicle mileage is 3,039,122 miles (4,890,992 km)—enough to circle Earth at the equator about 126 times!

3. False. In 1997, a car powered by a jet engine set the land speed record of 763 miles per hour (1,228 km/h)—faster than the speed of sound.

4. True. Early drivers used hand signals, which were hard to see at night, to indicate when they were stopping or turning left or right. Brake lights were added about 10 years after the first cars hit the road.

THRUST SSC CAR

INDEX

Bold page numbers refer to illustrations.

PHOTO CREDITS

Book produced by SCOUT
President and Editorial Director: Susan Knopf
Editor: Beth Adelman
Art Director and Designer:
Teresa Bonaddio, SparkerLit Studio LLC
Cover Consultant: Lucca Mattheus

GOOD HOUSEKEEPING INSTITUTE
Laurie Jennings, General Manager; Rachel Rothman, Chief Technologist & Executive Technical Director; Birnur K. Aral, Ph.D., Executive Director, Beauty, Health & Sustainability Lab; Carolyn E. Forté, Executive Director, Home Care & Cleaning Lab; Lexie Sachs, Executive Director, Textiles, Paper & Apparel Lab; Nicole Papantoniou, Director, Kitchen Appliances & Innovation Lab; Stefani Sassos, M.S., R.D.N., C.D.N., Deputy Director, Nutrition Lab; Dan Diclerico, Director, Home Improvement & Outdoor; Alec Scherma, Test Engineer; Nikolas Greenwald, Lab Assistant.

Published by Hearst Home Kids
An imprint of Hearst Books
Hearst Magazine Media, Inc.
300 W 57th Street
New York, NY 10019

For information about custom editions, special sales, premium and corporate purchases:
hearst.com/magazines/hearst-books

Printed in China

ISBN 978-1-958395-85-1